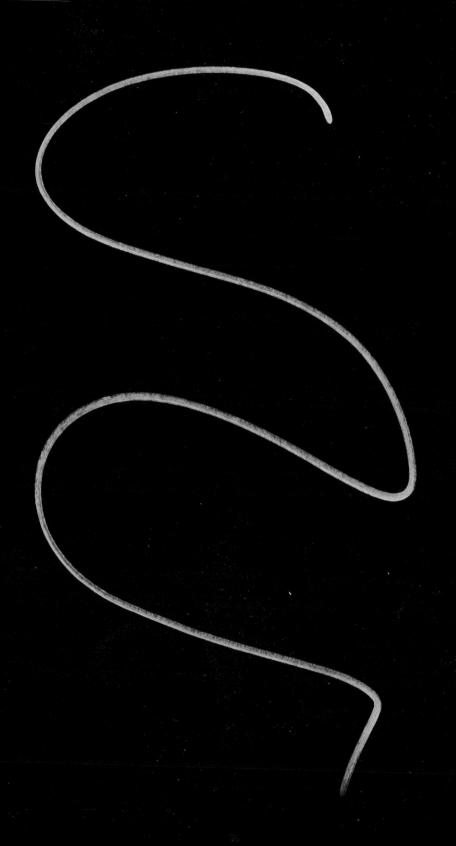

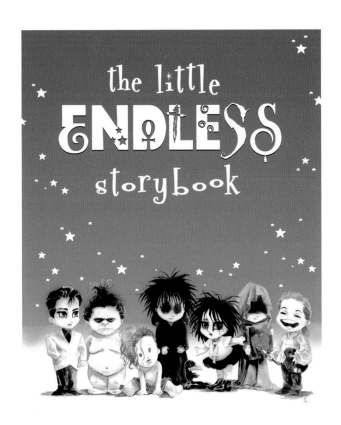

the little
ENDLESS
storybook

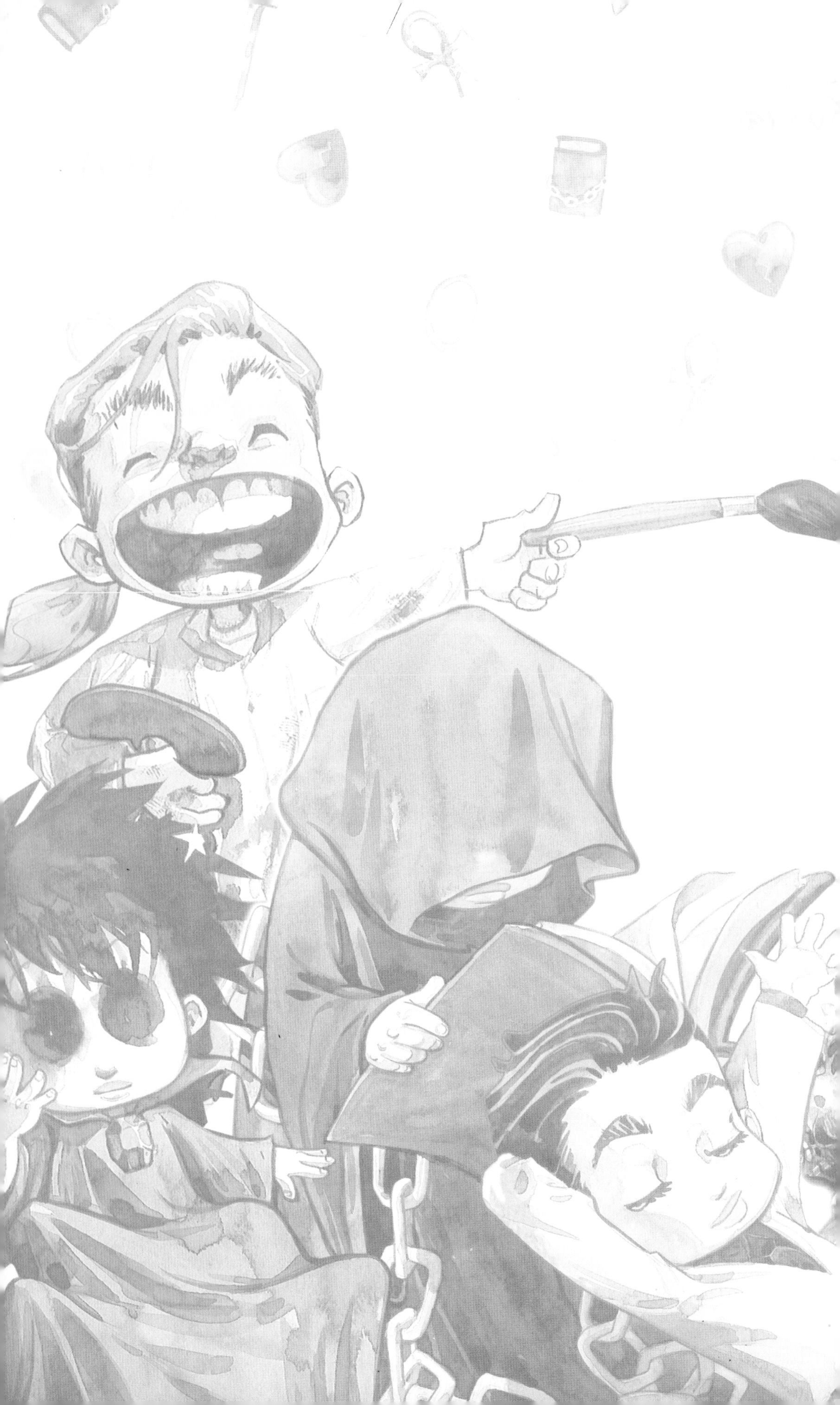

the little ENDLESS storybook

by JILL THOMPSON

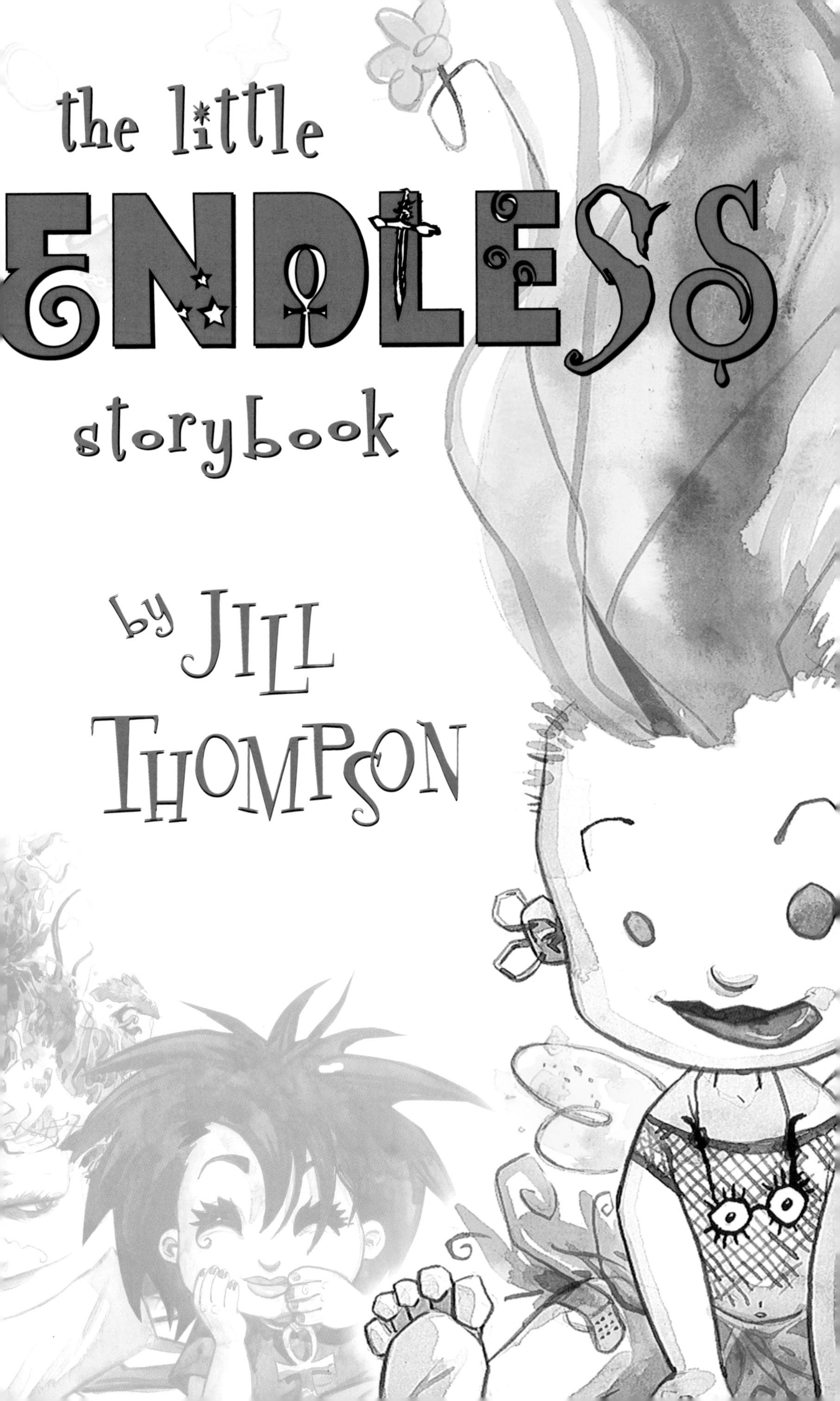

Karen Berger SVP-EXECUTIVE EDIT

Shelly Bond EDIT

Angela Rufino ASSOCIATE EDIT

Robbin Brosterman DESIGN DIRECTOR-BOO

Curtis King SENIOR ART DIRECT

DC COMIC

Diane Nelson PRESIDE

Dan DiDio and Jim Lee CO-PUBLISHE

Geoff Johns CHIEF CREATIVE OFFIC

Patrick Caldon EVP-FINANCE AND ADMINISTRATI

John Rood EVP-SALES, MARKETING AND BUSINESS DEVELOPME

Amy Genkins SVP-BUSINESS AND LEGAL AFFAI

Steve Rotterdam SVP-SALES AND MARKETI

John Cunningham VP-MARKETI

Terri Cunningham VP-MANAGING EDIT

Alison Gill VP-MANUFACTURI

David Hyde VP-PUBLIC

Sue Pohja VP-BOOK TRADE SAI

Alysse Soll VP-ADVERTISING AND CUSTOM PUBLISHI

Bob Wayne VP-SAL

Mark Chiarello ART DIRECT

Neil Gaiman, consulta

Painted cover by Jill Thomps

Endless Logo Design by Nancy Oga

Publication design by Amie Brockway-Metca

Photo of Jill Thompson by DAN

The Sandman is created
Gaiman, Kieth and Dringenbe

THE LITT
ENDLESS STORYBOO
Published
DC Comics, 1700 Broadw
New York, NY 100
Copyright © 2001, 20
DC Comics. Afterwo
Copyright © 2004 DC Comi
All Rights Reserved. VERTIC
and all characters featured
this publication, the distincti
likenesses thereof and related elemen
are trademarks of DC Comics. The storie
characters and incidents featured in th
publication are entirely fictional. DC Comics do
not read or accept unsolicited submissio
of ideas, stories or artwor

Printed in the U.S.A. Second Printi
DC Comics, a Warner Bros. Entertainment Compa
ISBN: 978-1-4012-0428-

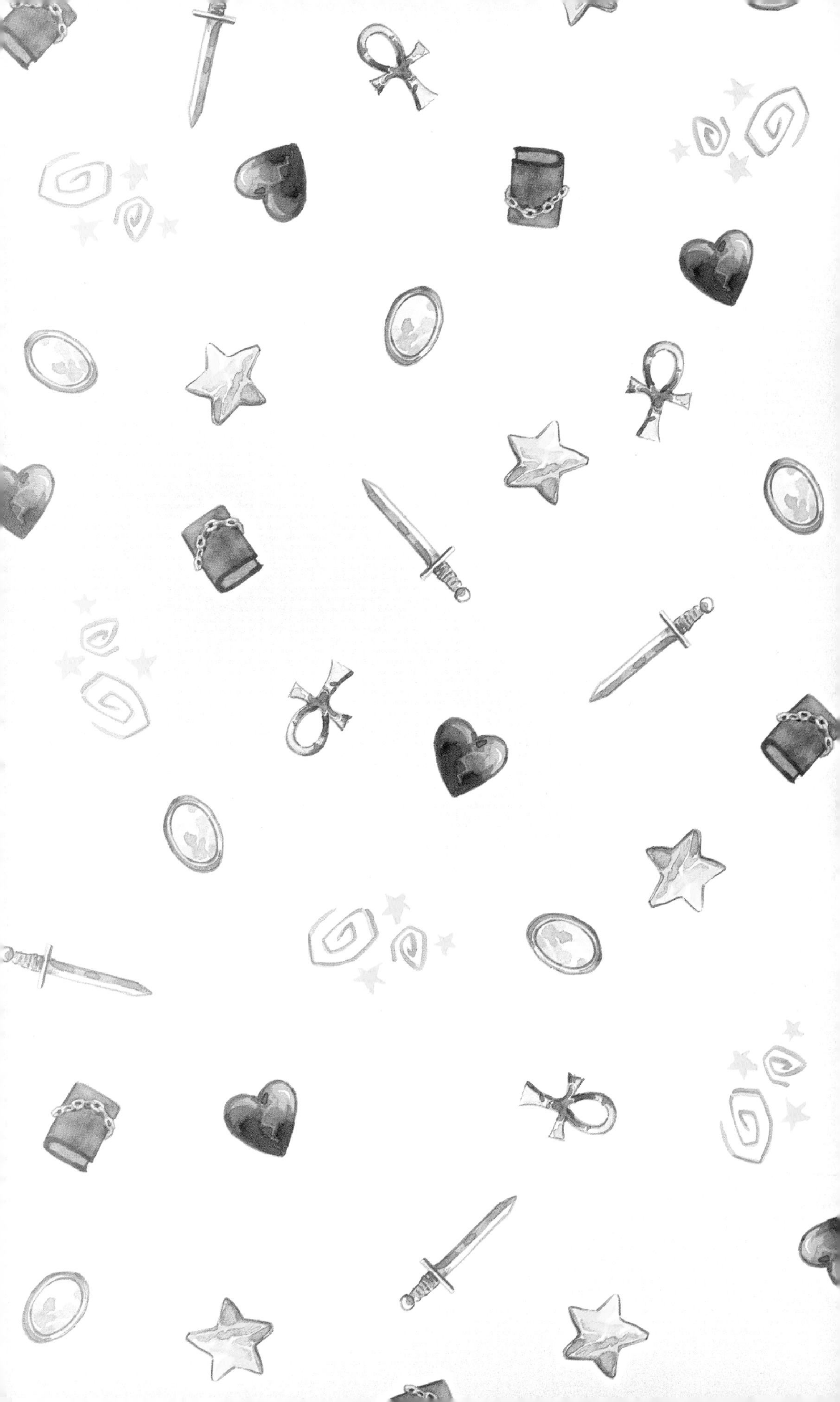

Once upon a time, in an ice-cream-colored realm,
there lived a tiny little princess named Delirium and her dog Barnabas.

It was Barnabas' job to look after the princess
because she was very easily distracted and often got lost
if she went out walking by herself.

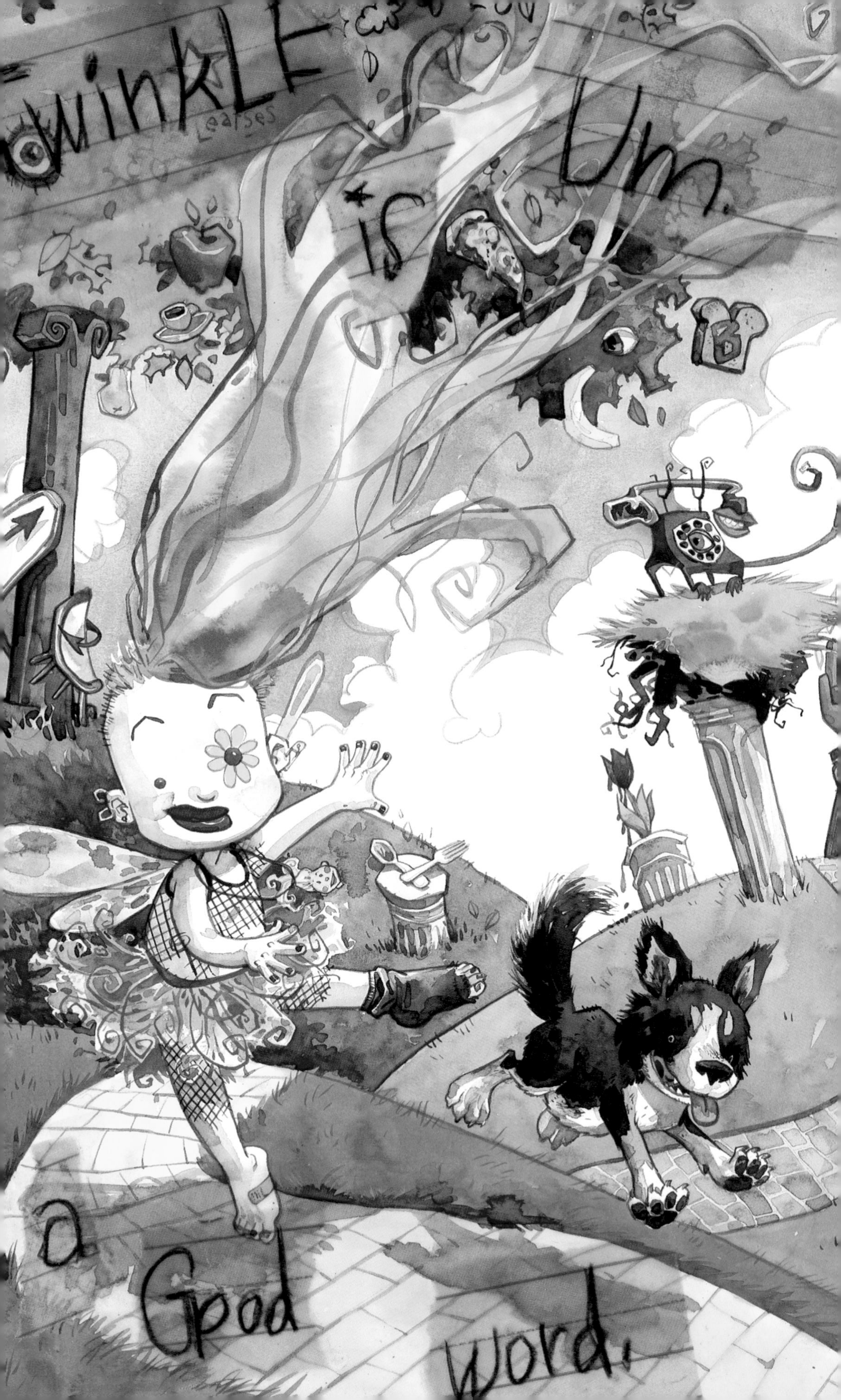

winkLE is Um.
a Good word.

On a pistachio day, Delirium and Barnabas went out wandering.
They sniffed the music and tasted the words
that were particularly crispy on the tongue, like *twinkle* and *citrus*.

And they walked. And walked and walked and walked.

And then they walked some more.

Soon Barnabas turned to the little princess and said,
"Um...listen, kiddo, I've gotta see a man about a tree...if you get my drift."

"I know a treeman," replied Delirium. "His name is Ghillie Dhu
and he's all leafsie and green but he doesn't drift like I can.
Are you taking him a harvest pie?"

" Um, riiight." humored the pup.
"Why don't you sit right here, on this very spot, Delirium.
And don't move. I'll be back in a flash."

"Okay!" giggled Delirium as Barnabas tore off into the foliage.

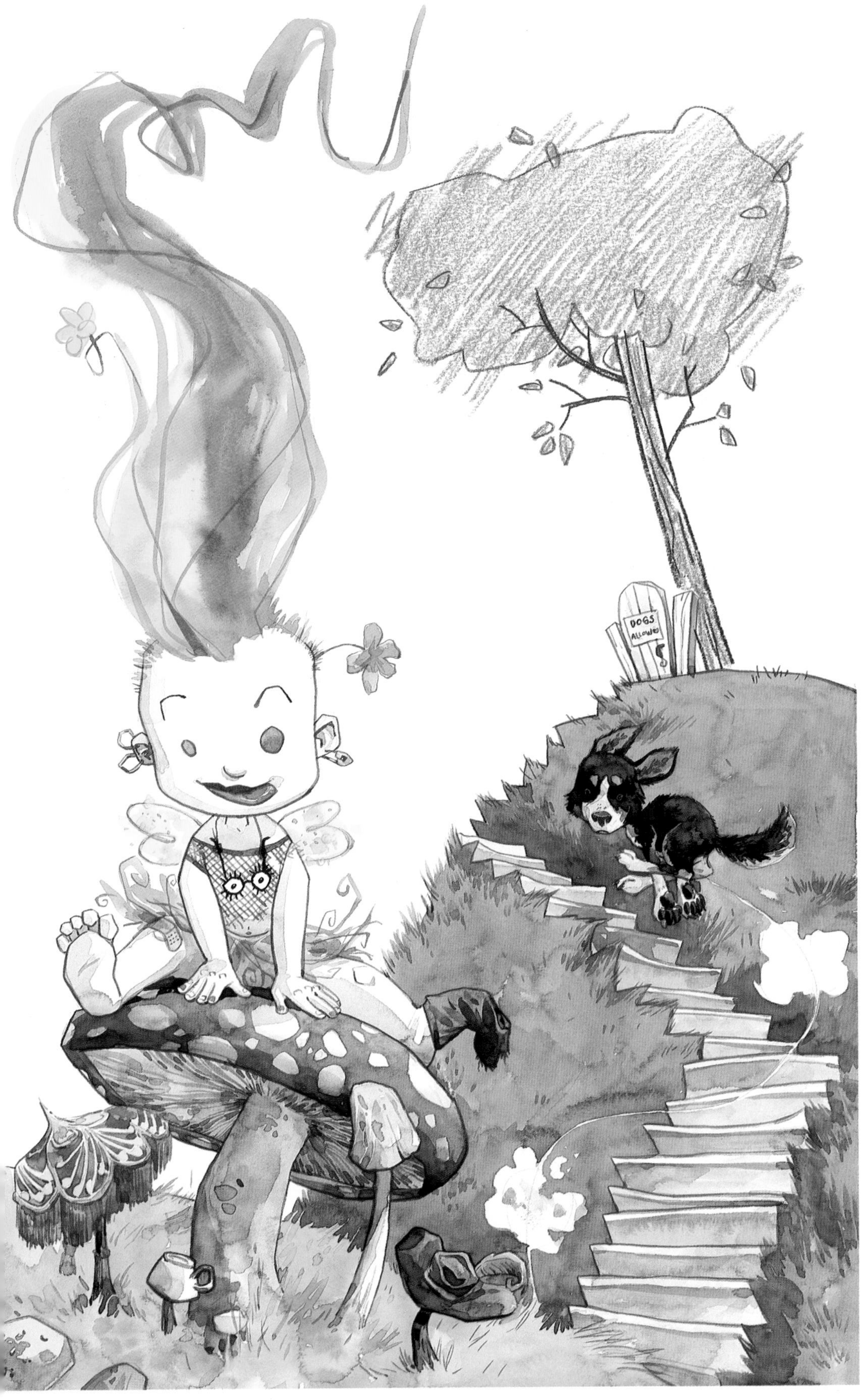
DOGS
ALLOWED

"I like the moss people, too, don't you, puppy? Um. Puppy?"

The littlest princess blinked her glittery eyes and to her surprise, there was no Barnabas by her side.

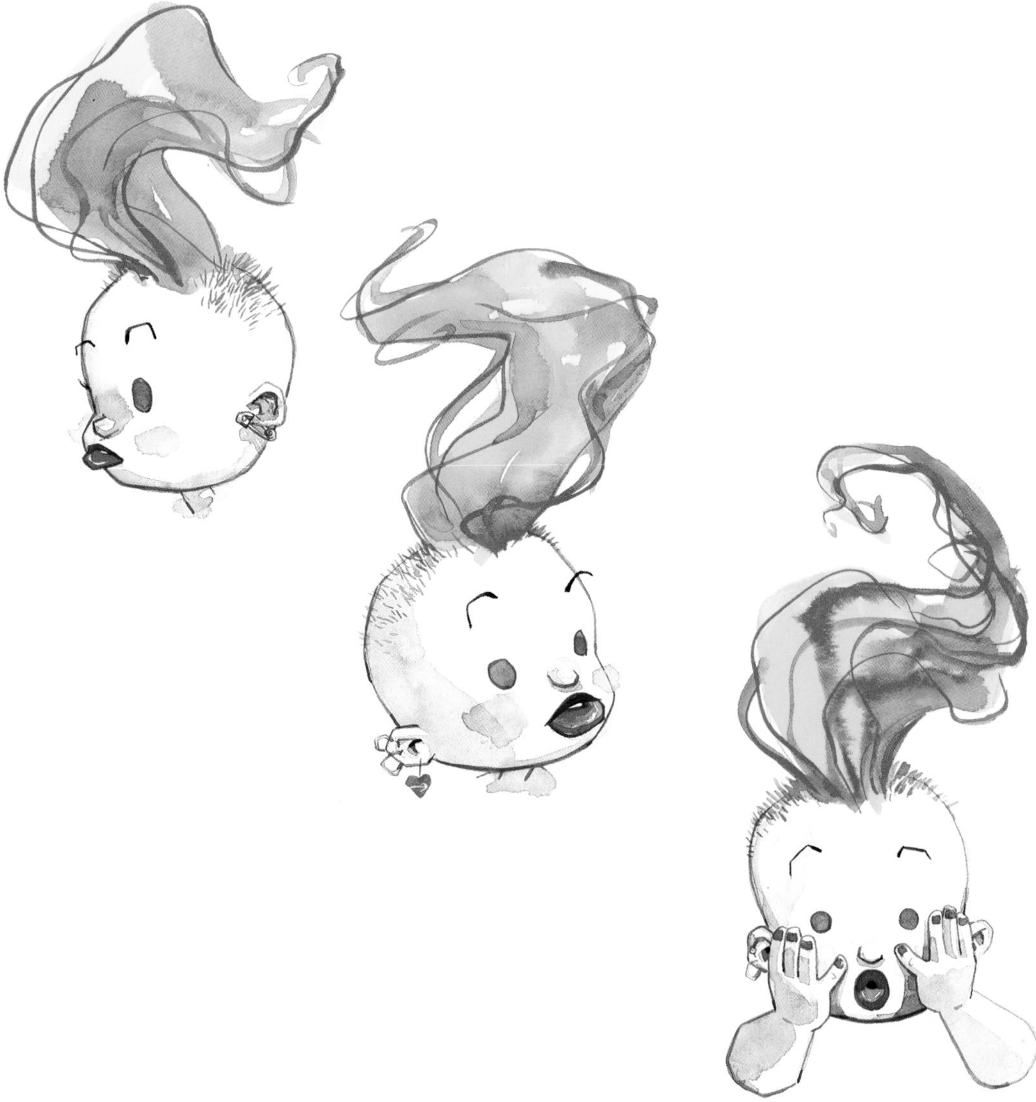

"Oh, no!" cried Delirium. "My doggie has wandered away! He's all losted! He must be very frightened. Don't worry, I'm coming to get you, Mr. Losty MacLosty."

And she fluttered off to find her puppy.

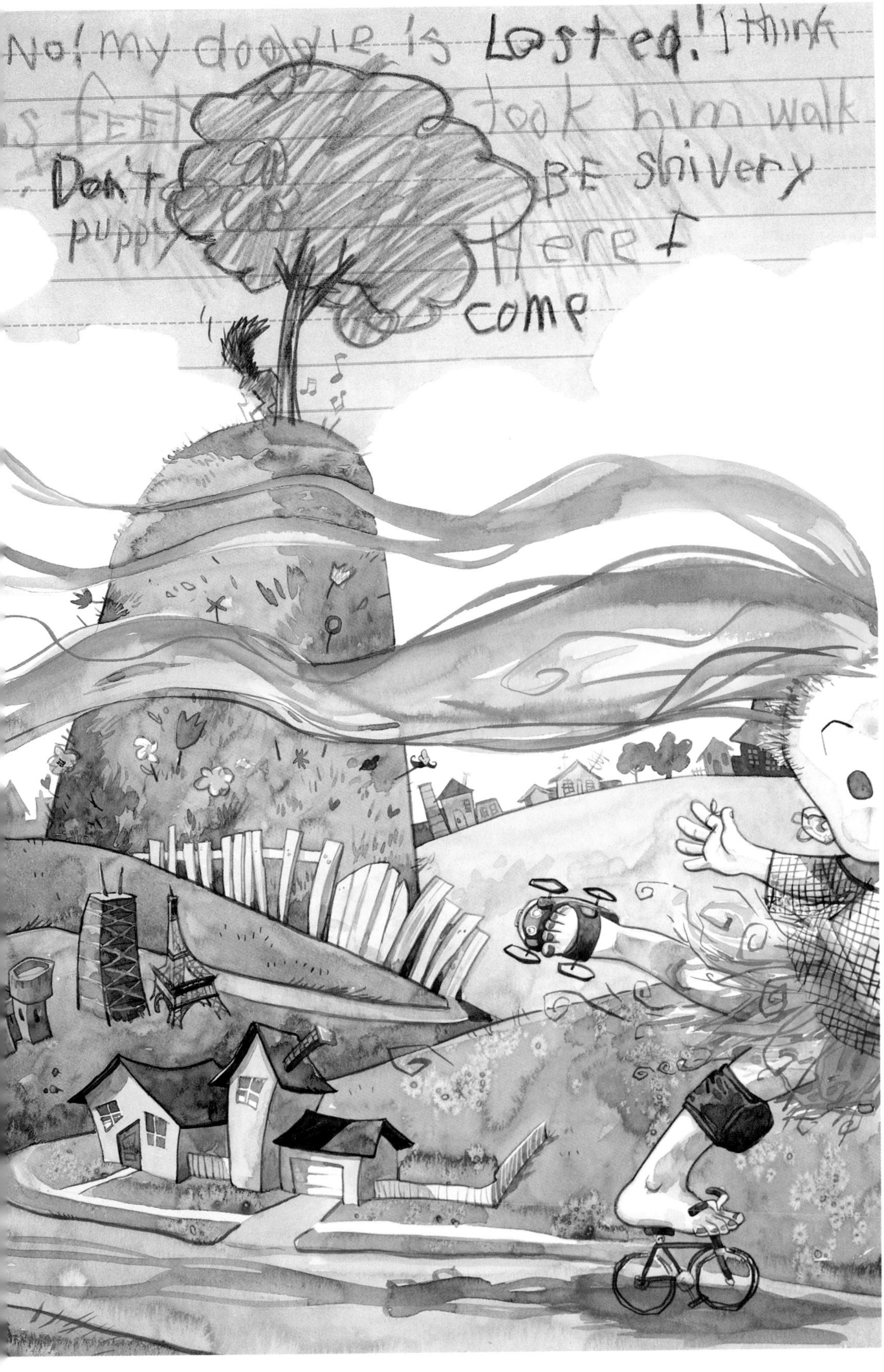
No! my doggie is Losted! I think
took him walk
Don't
BE shivery
puppy
Here I
come

His business completed,
Barnabas scampered back to the empty spot
where Delirium once was.

"Aw, nuts!" he yipped. "Not again!"
And Barnabas padded off to find his girlie.

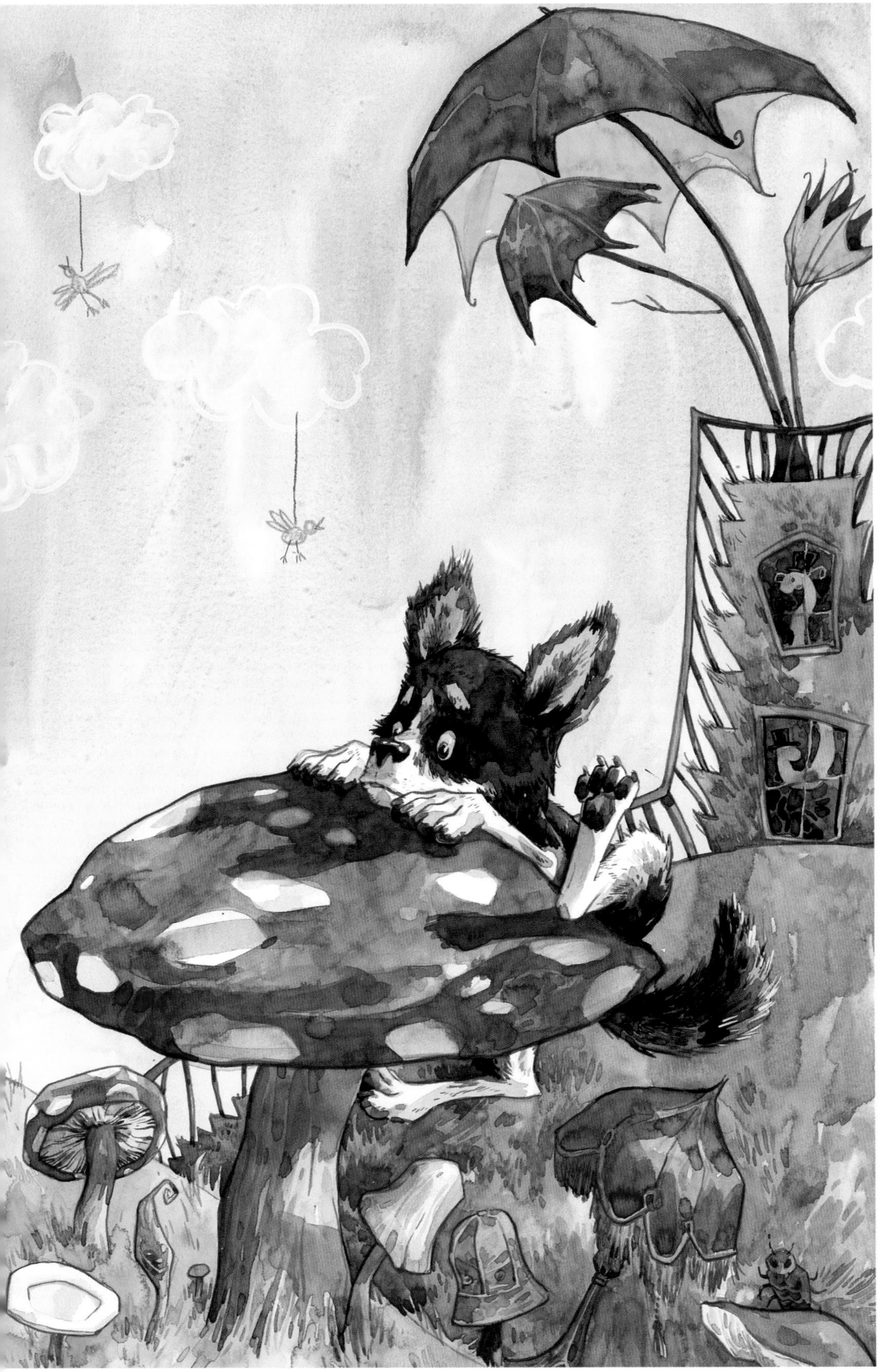

He looked in all the places
he thought a Technicolor princess might like to be.

The open air market, for example...
with its baubles and books and bangles and beads.

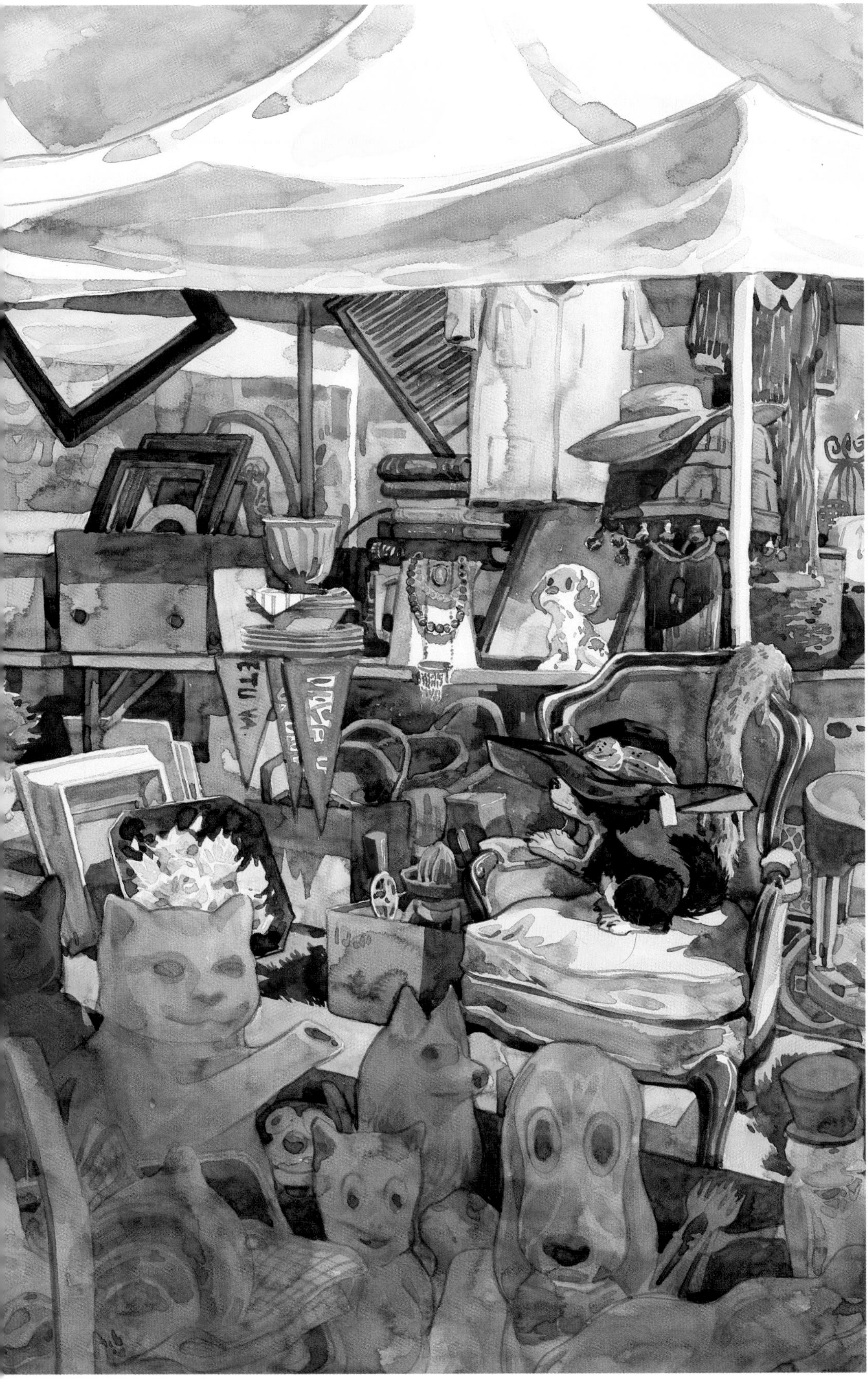

Or perhaps the ocean...
where the waves crash upon the shore
with a deafening roar.

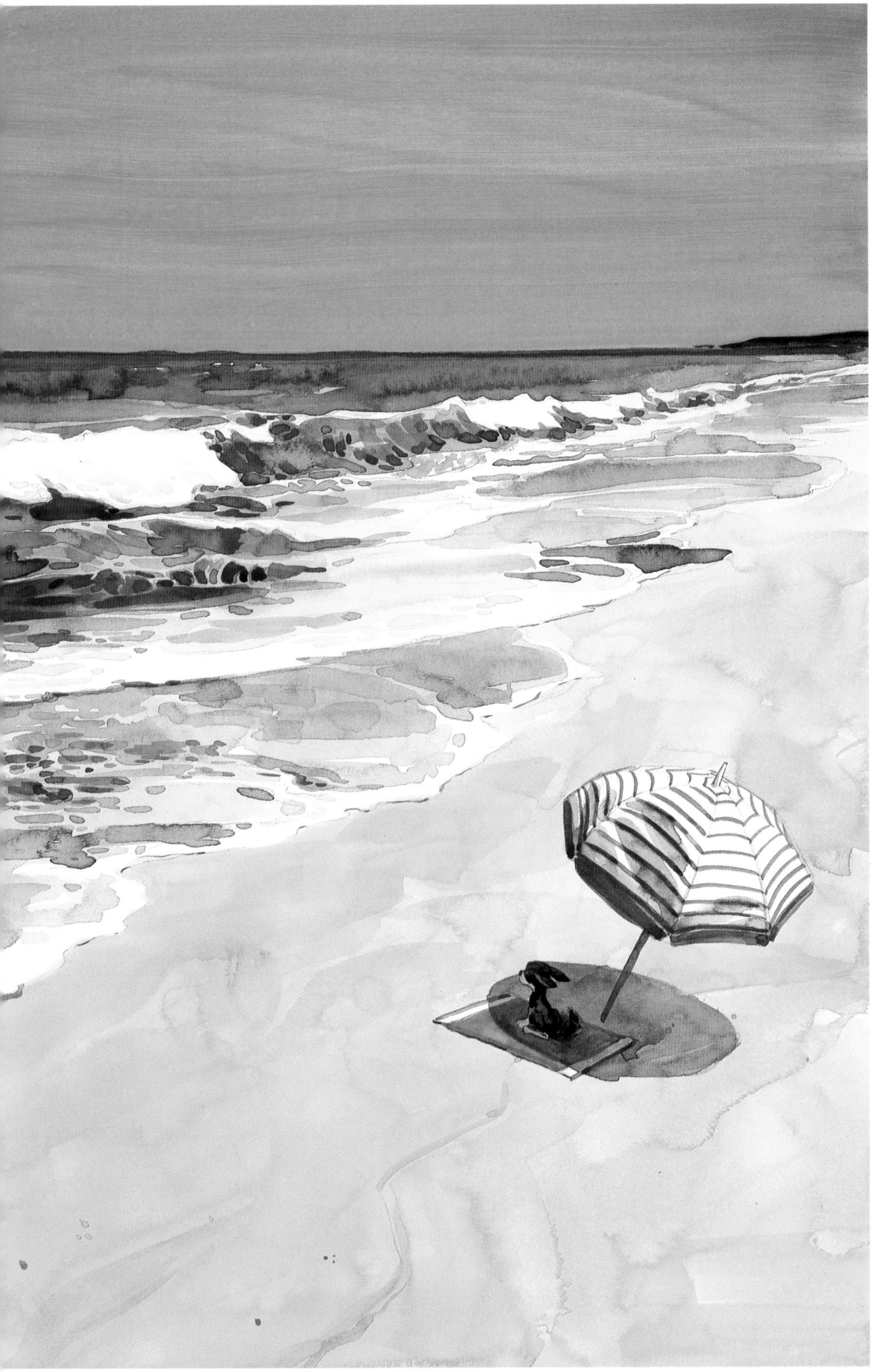

Or the pastry shop...
filled with delectable creations of sugar and cream.

But the princess was in none of these places.

Barnabas put his paw to his nose and thought for a while.
"Hey! I know. I'll go ask her brothers and sisters!
She's got six of them. One of them should know where Delirium would go!"

And away he ran, as fast as his fuzzy legs could carry him.

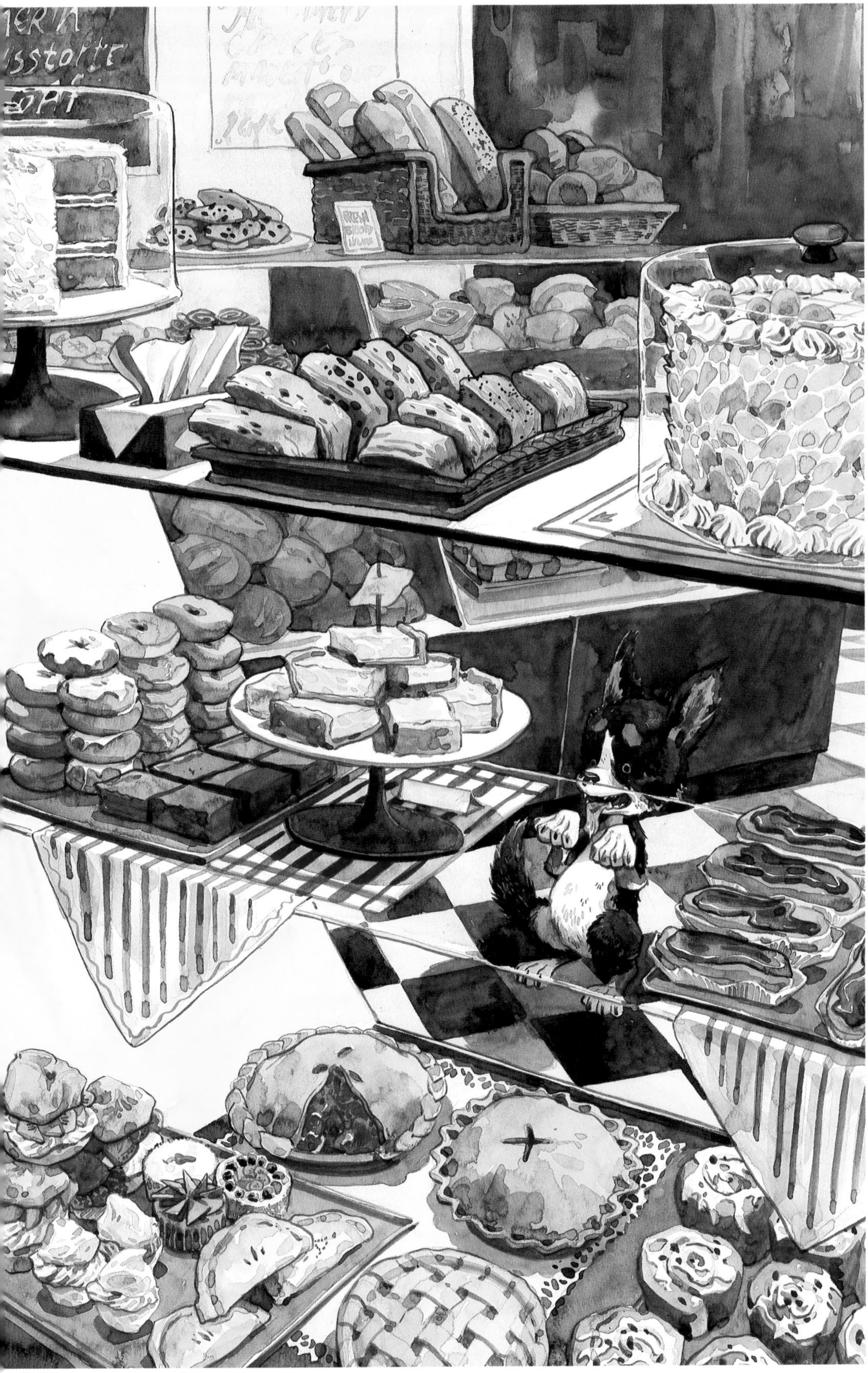

Delirium's older brother Destruction lived in a house very far away—almost at the edge of everything. Barnabas trotted up to the edge of a deep, thick forest. He would have to travel through the Woods between the Worlds if he wished to find his friend. And it seemed there was no path.

"Gosh, these woods are dark and twisty. If I get lost, I'll never be able to find little Del." The puppy put his paw to his nose and thought for a moment.

"Ha! I've got it!" he barked and then slipped into the shadows.

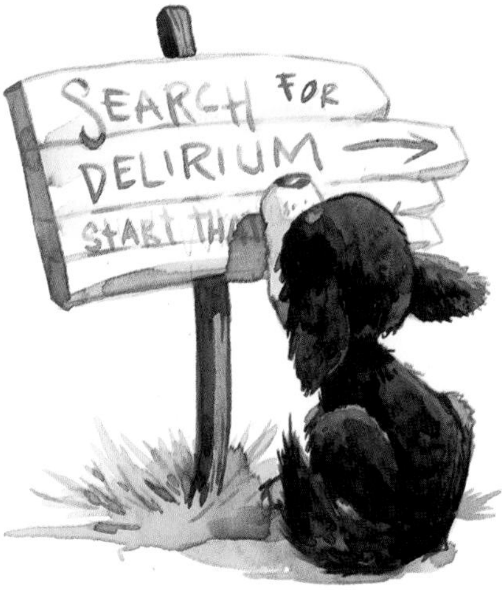
SEARCH FOR
DELIRIUM

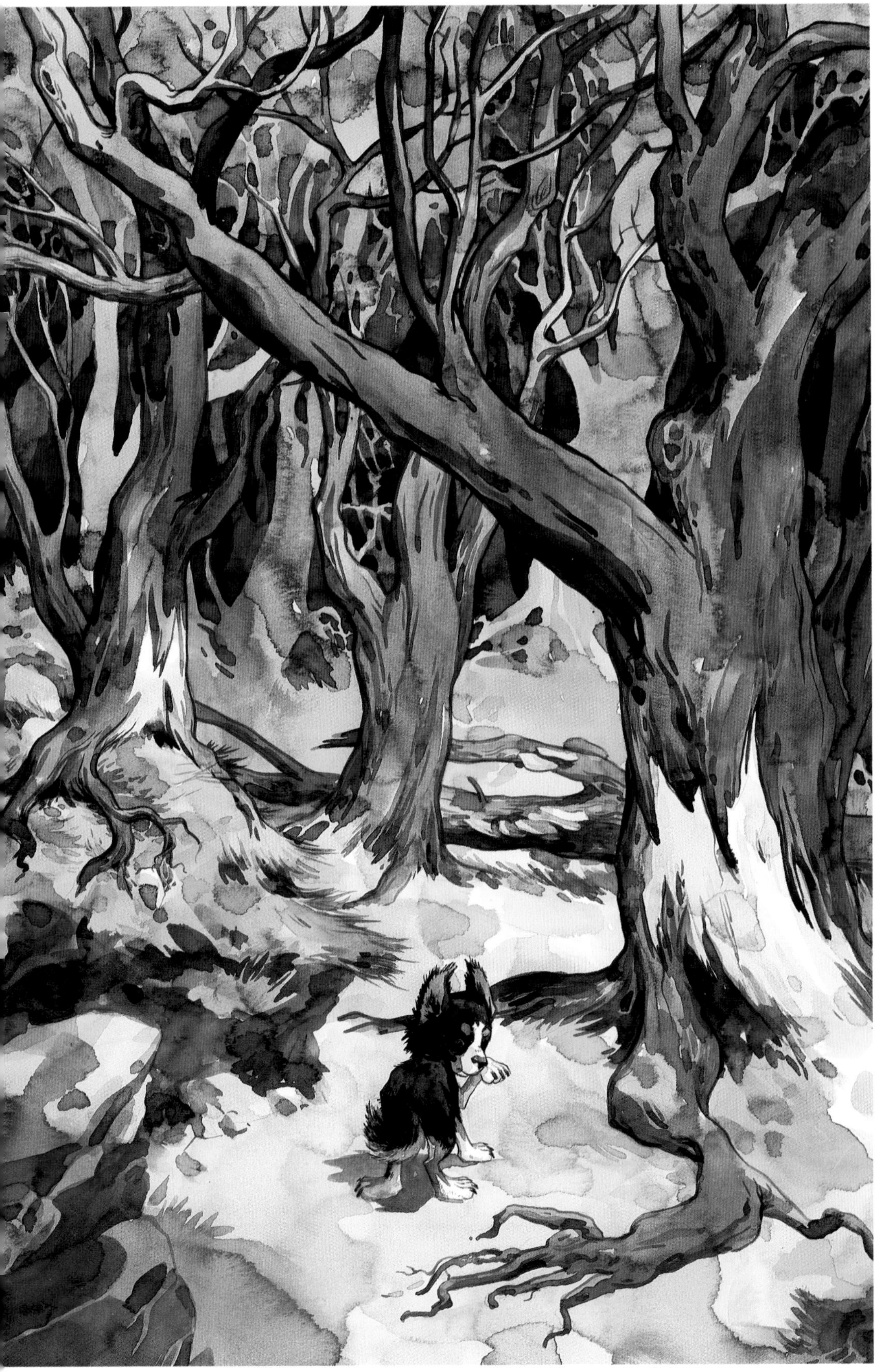

Our hero Barnabas bounded from tree to tree
and left a little mark on each one.
That way, if he got lost, he'd be able to tell which way he'd already been.
He wagged his tail because he was so clever.
"What do I have to fear from gnarly trees?
After all, I'm a dog...and dogs and trees go together like..."

"Wha...What was that?"

Out of the corner of his eye, Barnabas saw a shape behind him.
Then, in an instant, it was gone.

"Um, maybe it's not trees in the woods that I should be worried about,"
thought Barnabas. "It's the *things* that live in the woods.
Things that might not like dogs marking up their trees!"
But Barnabas was the protector of the Lady Delirium
and he had to be brave to find her.

So he tucked his tail between his legs and said in a very loud voice
(which would certainly impress and intimidate Foresty Things),
"I am the guardian of the princess Delirium...and um,
I hereby bestow upon these trees the...um...Canine...Seal of Excellentness!"

And then he sprinted out of the forest.

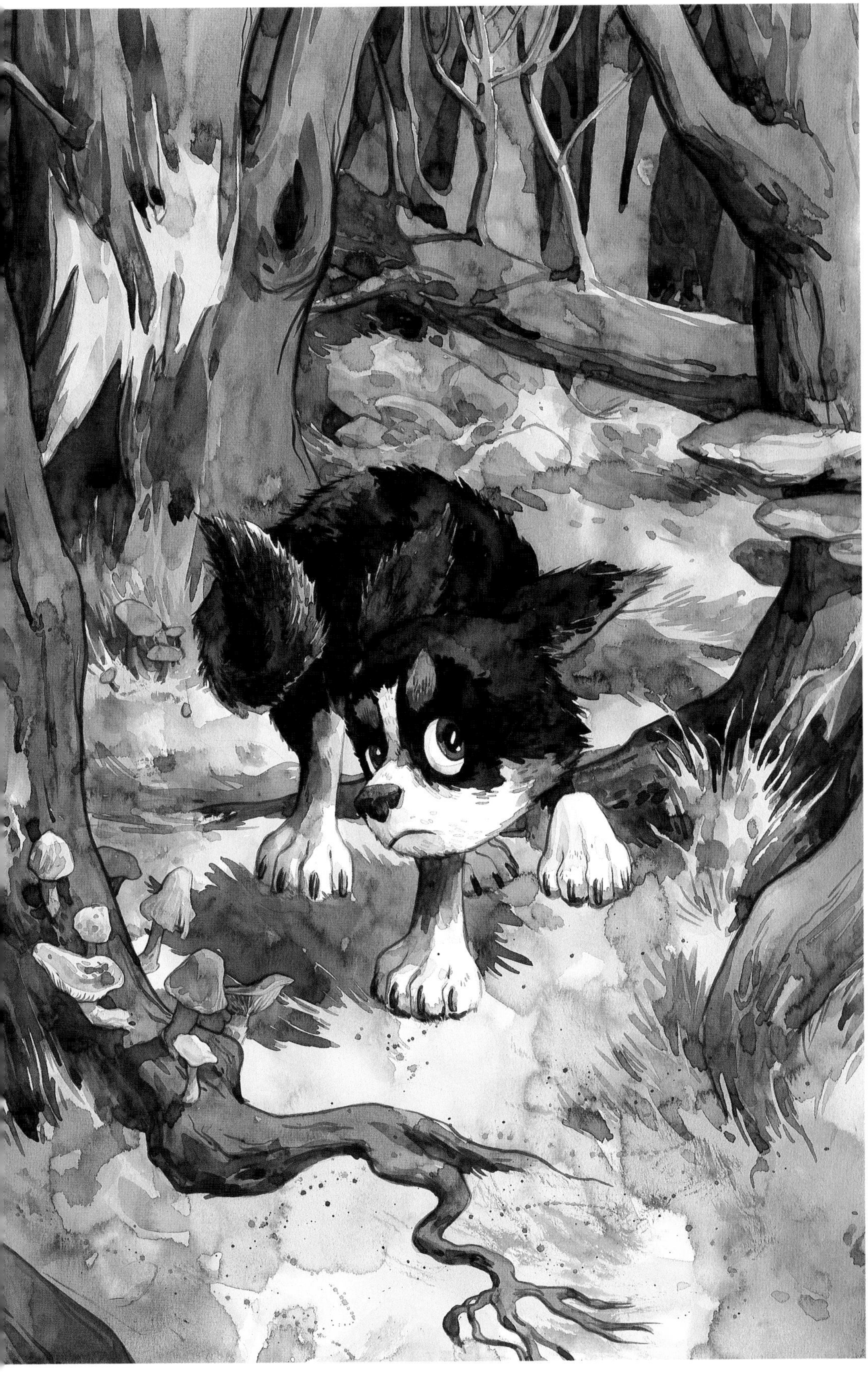

Barnabas ran and ran until he found himself
at the bottom of a steep cliff.
High above he would find the house of Delirium's older brother Destruction.
He dug his nails into the side of the cliff
and used his teeth to hold onto roots as he climbed to the top.

"If you didn't have to hold on for dear life with your face,
it would probably be a nice view..." he commented to himself.

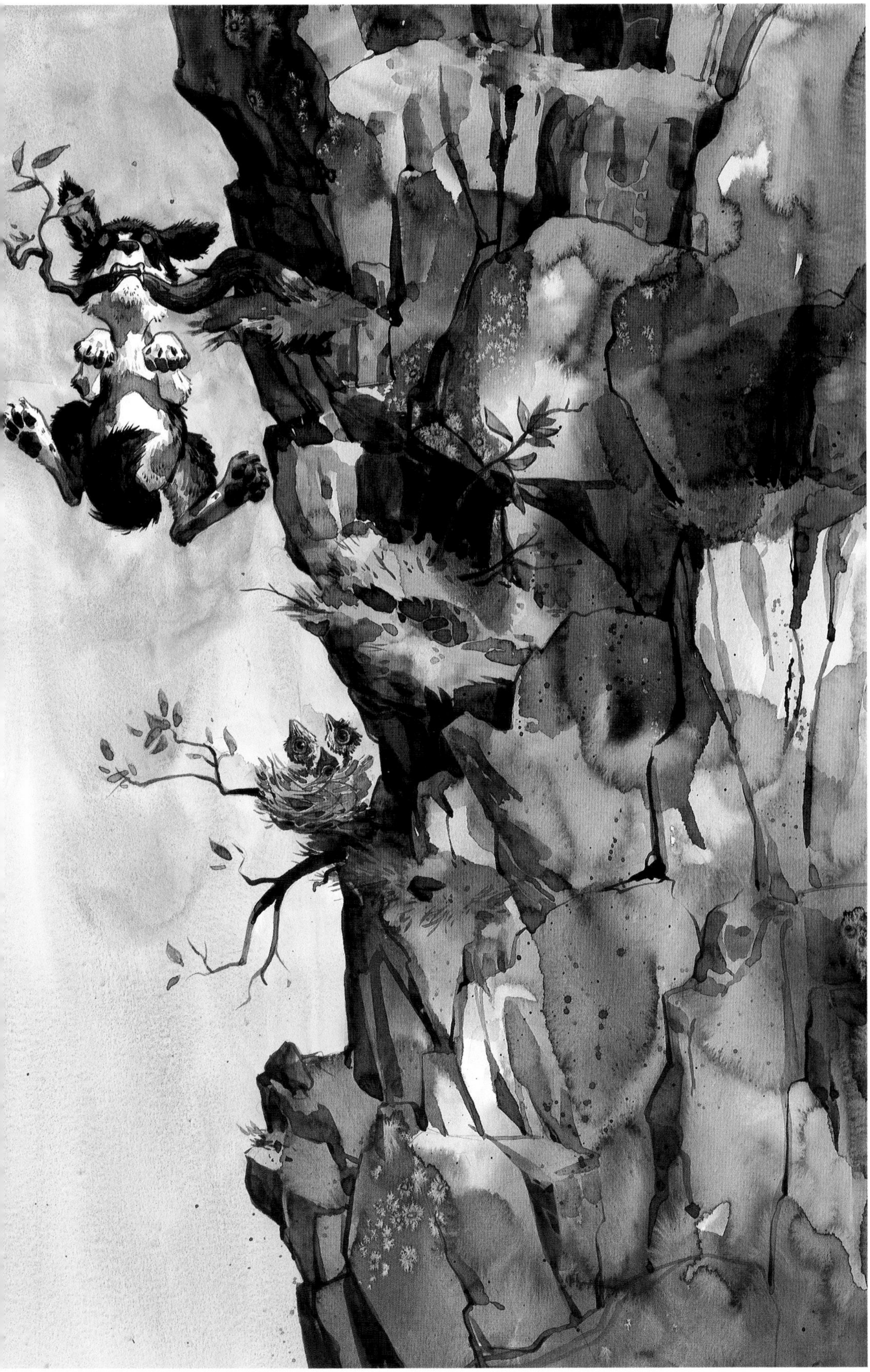

"Didja ever think about putting in some stairs?"
Barnabas said when he reached Delirium's brother,
who was painting at the cliff's edge.

"HA HA HA!" laughed the older brother from behind his canvas.
"Where would the challenge be in that?"
The brother shouted over the side. "Sister! Are you still climbing?"

Barnabas looked down at his paws and spit some root out of his mouth.
"Um, that's kinda what I was here to talk to you about, my Lord.
I was hoping that your little sister might be with you...
I fear I have...uh...*misplaced* her."

"WHAT?" roared the oldest brother.
"I thought I told you to watch over her!
You know how easily distracted she can be."
The brother furrowed his brow and thought a bit.

"Hmmm, well, she is not in my realm so she is all in one piece.
I suggest you ask our oldest brother."

Then Destruction reached into his pocket. "Here, take this."
It was a wee little charm in the shape of a sword.
"It will help you with my sister."

"T'anks!" the puppy said, and then ran off with the charm in his mouth.

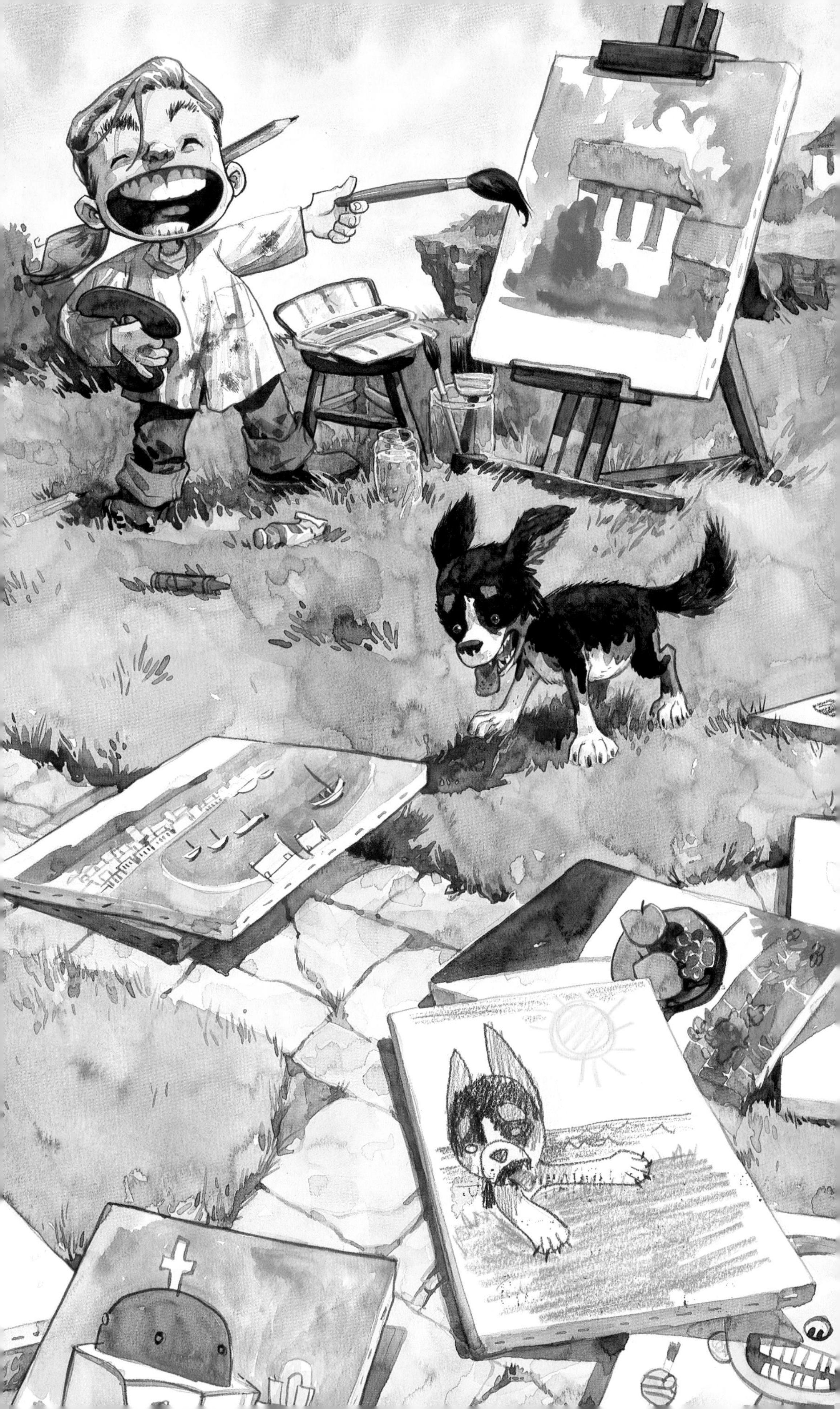

Soon Barnabas came to a wild, overgrown garden maze.
He knew that he'd find the next brother's realm at the center of it.
He trotted through the hedgerows, taking care to avoid the prickly brambles.
He navigated his way around corner after corner
and only once did he come to a dead end.

"No time to go back!" he said as he wagged his tail and dug under the bush.
Through the hole he could see the giant statues that decorated
the brother's garden. "I'm almost there!" he shouted, "Terrific! I'll…"

"What was that?"
Barnabas thought he saw something behind him again,
like the mysterious Thing from the forest.
It seemed to jump from side to side.

"It must have followed me! Darn! I had to mention 'princess' in the forest…
I shoulda realized everyone wants a piece of the royal family!
Well, you're not following me to Delirium, bud!" the puppy grumbled.
And then he tucked his paws and tail under himself and
squeezed beneath the bush.

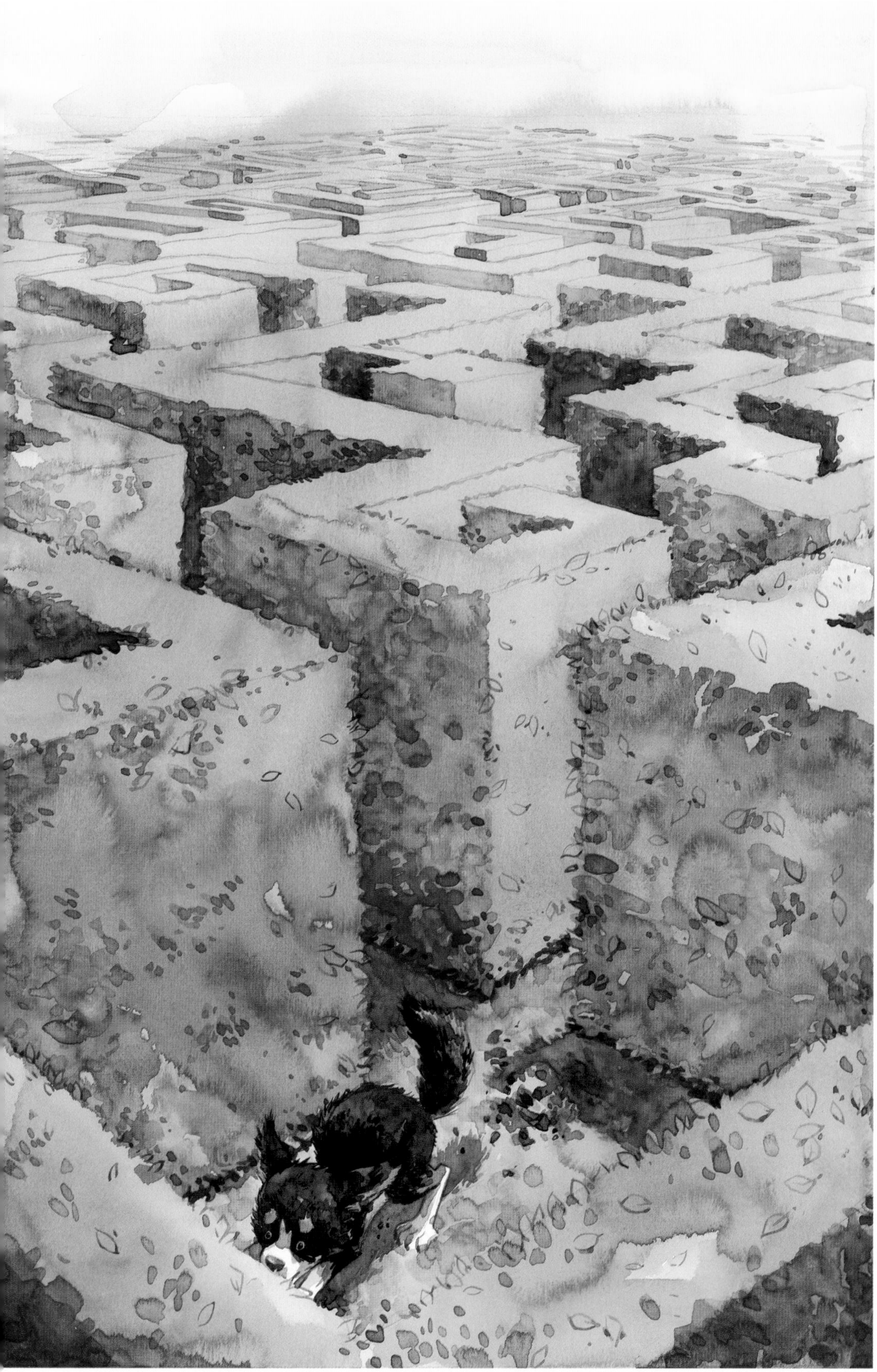

The determined canine popped out on the other side
to find himself standing in a misty garden with many paths.
Delirium's brother Destiny stood on the walkway
reading from his enormous book.

Before Barnabas could speak,
the brother whispered from under his hooded robe,
"Little dog, there are no pages in my book that state my sister is lost.
I suggest you visit our sister."

"But, I didn't even..." stammered Barnabas.
The tiny sword dropped from his mouth and onto the path
in front of Destiny. Delirium's brother picked up the charm
and added a tiny version of his ancient book to it.

"It is written in the book that this will help you with our sister."
And with that he glided silently down the path.

Barnabas put the charms in his mouth
and headed out of the garden.

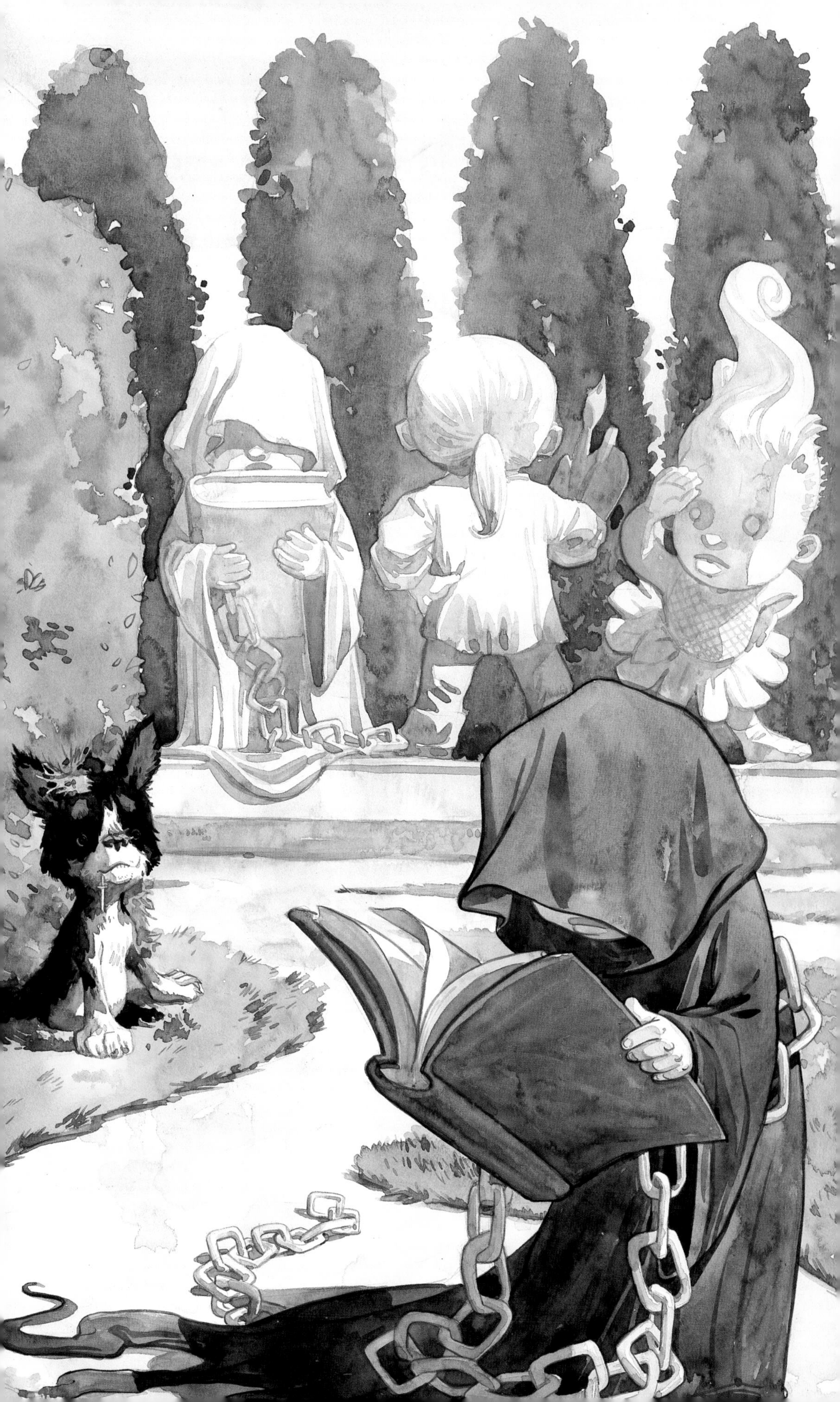

As he walked, it became more and more difficult for Barnabas to see.
The garden had turned into a thick, soupy fog.
Barnabas sniffed the air and was pleased
when he detected Delirium's sister's scent in the distance.
He wagged his tail and sniffed again, trying to determine the direction.
"Smells like wet leaves, she does...

"What's that?"

Barnabas thought as he caught a quick glimpse of the "something"
in the fog behind him. "Can't let it get to my lucky charms!"
He tucked his tail under himself for proper aerodynamics
and zoomed off as quickly as he could.

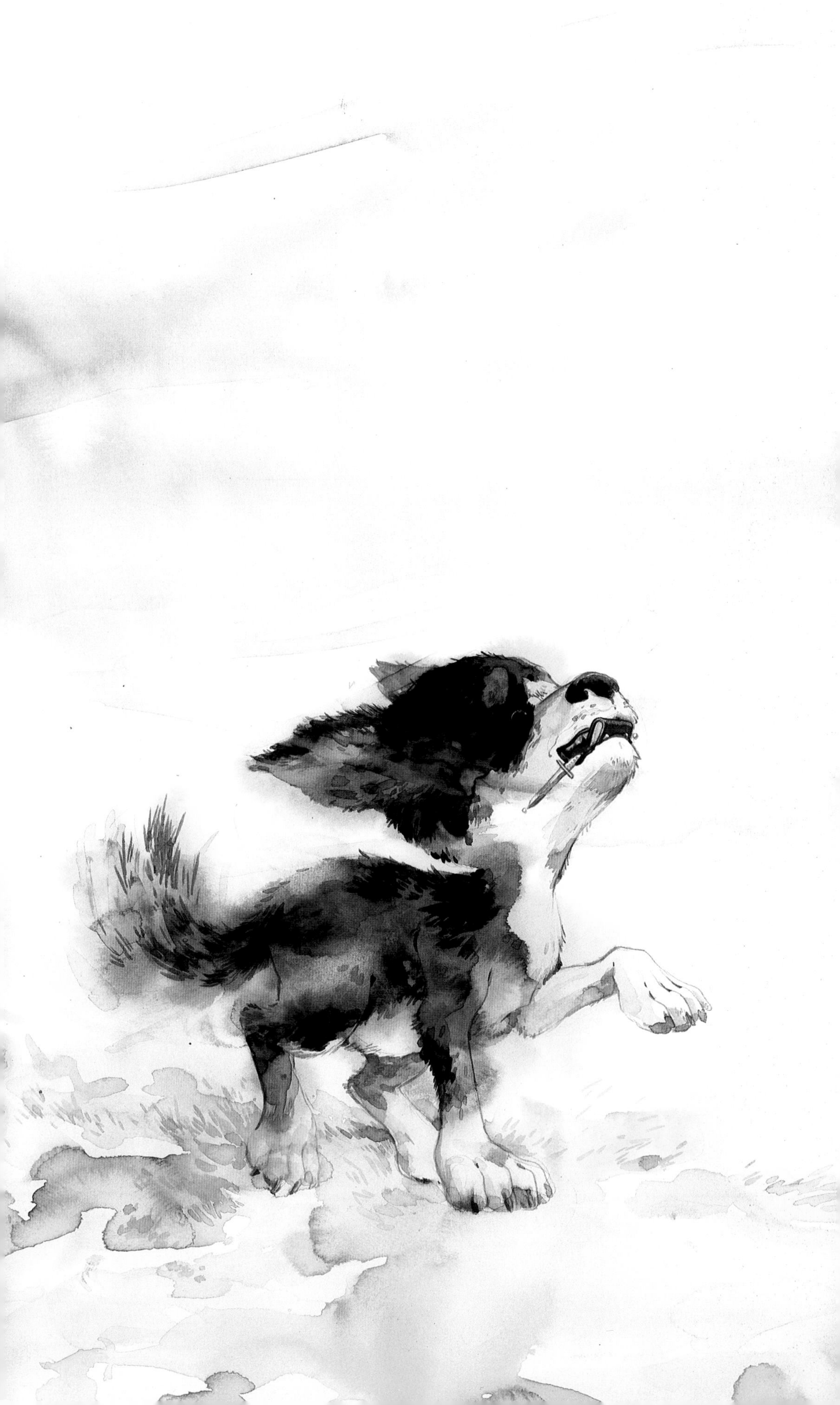

"Run! Run! As fast as you can! You can't catch me I'm...OOOOOOW!"
Barnabas howled as he suddenly smashed
into something wide and squooshy in the fog.

He looked up and stared into the face of Despair, Delirium's large, grim sister.
Hanging all around Despair in her realm were mirrors of every shape and size,
but none reflected Barnabas when he looked into them.
Despair snuffed and grunted at the dog as he cleared his head.
Rats ran up her limbs and settled into her nest of hair.

"M-my lady?" shivered Barnabas,
"H-have you run across the L-Lady Deliriumum in this fog?
Or have you s-seen her in one of your s-sad mirrors?"

"Little one," grumfed the squat sister,
"Delirium still has joy in her heart so she is not here with me in my realm..."

"But, take this...it will help you with our sister."

And she added a tiny mirrored charm to the others that Barnabas carried.

"Does this do magic or something?" asked the confused little pup.

" I suggest you ask our sister-brother," replied Despair.

"Yeah, yeah..." mumbled Barnabas as he journeyed on into the fog.

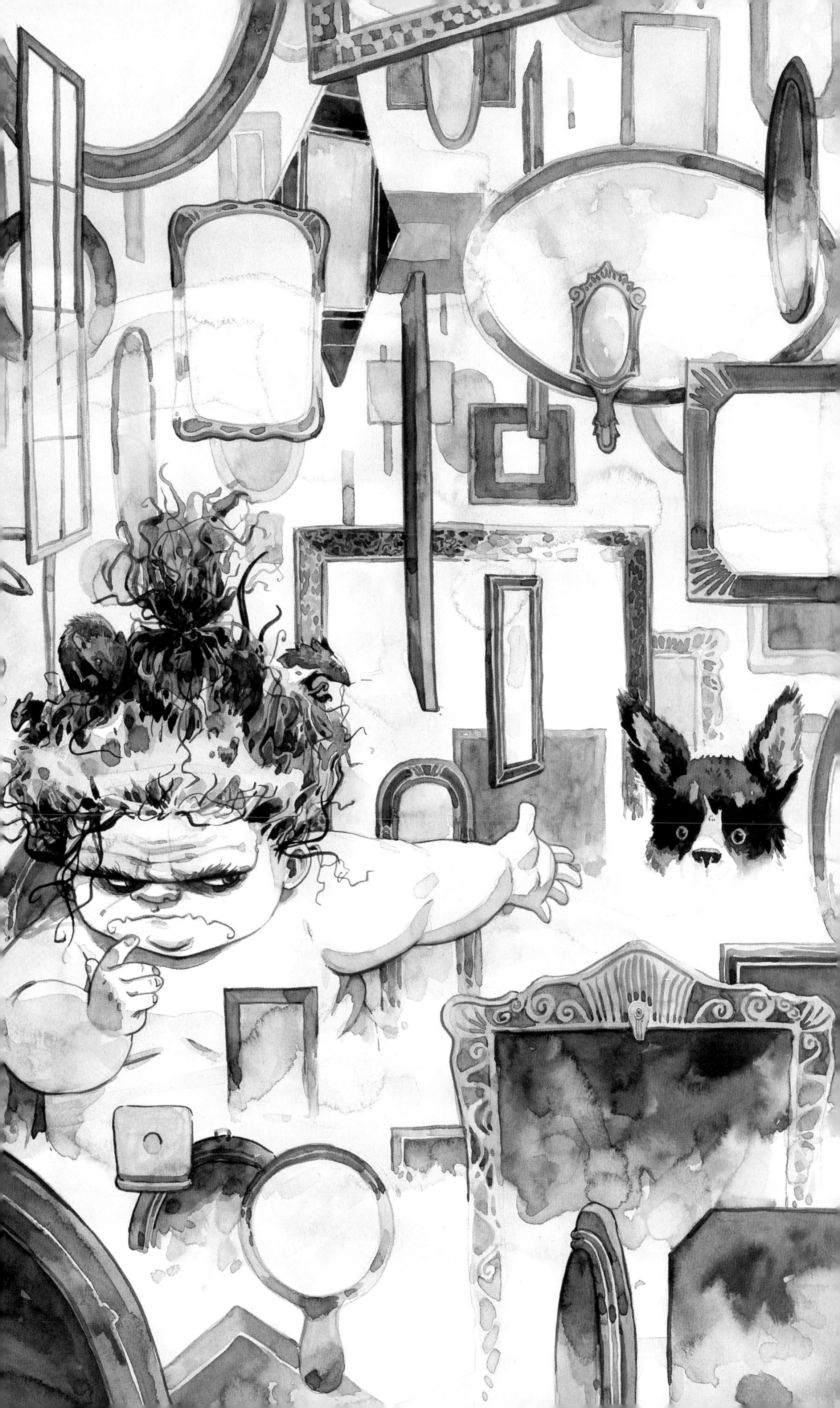

The fog carried him to the base of a staircase
that reached high into the sky. It seemed to go on forever.
But he was on a quest for the princess and if he had to climb
for a whole year to find her, then that's what he would do.

His nails clik-clicketied on the marble stairs as he began his long ascent.

"Don't any of these guys live someplace normal or easy to reach?
Like a nice house with a yard for guardians of princesses to frolic in?
Yeesh!" And he wagged his tail to the tune his toenails tapped.

"What was that?"
thought Barnabas as something flashed quickly behind him.
"That creepy Thing has followed me again! It's gotta be the paparazzi!
I'll bet they want the scoop on these magic charms.
Well, eat my dust, news hounds!" He pushed back his ears and
tucked in his tail and galloped up the stairs three at a time
until he disappeared into the heart of the door.

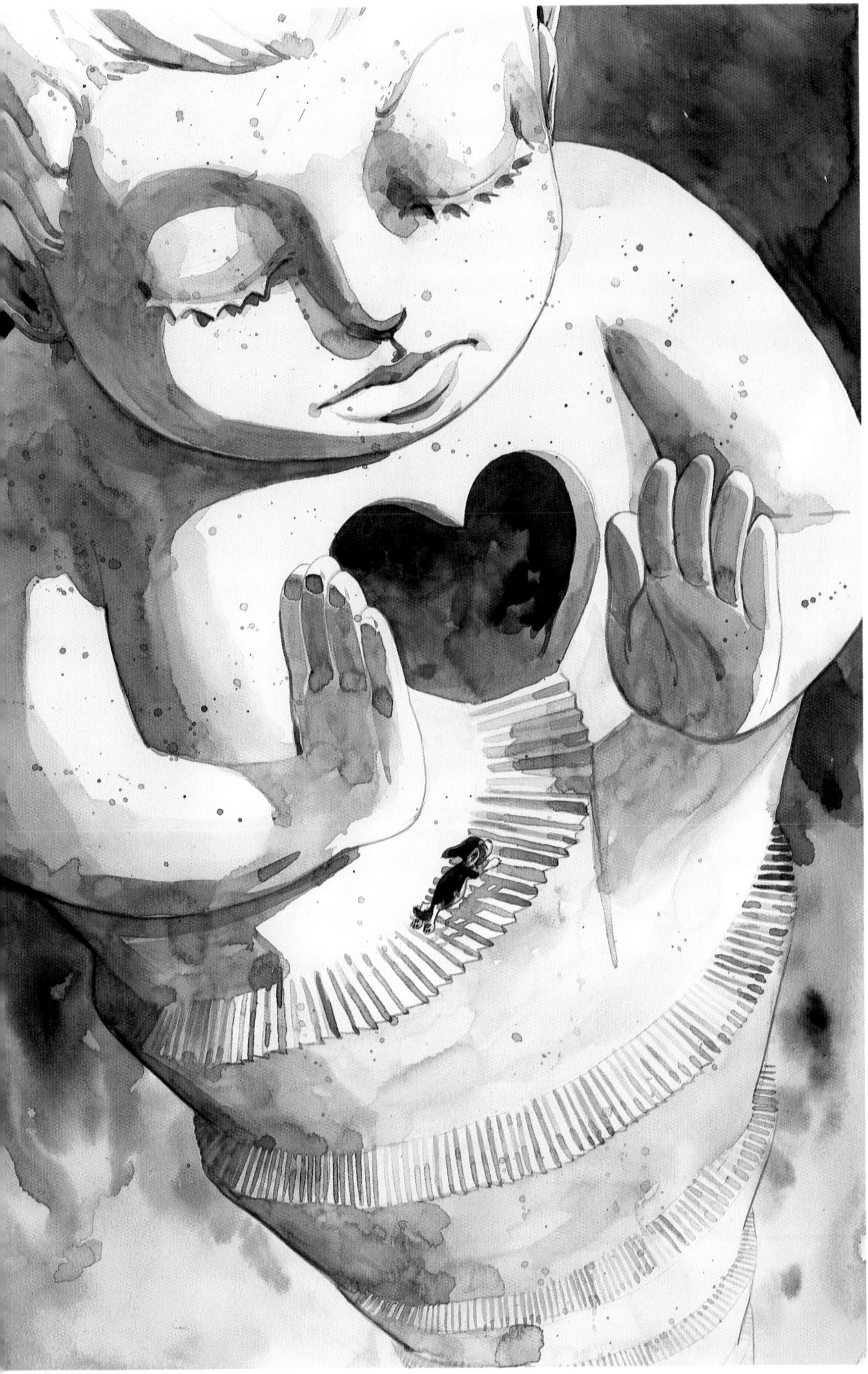

$\mathcal{B}$arnabas skittled across the floor of the throne room and slid to a stop.

Delirium's sibling Desire glanced down from its perch
upon the spongy red décor.

Barnabas gasped, "I've been here! I've been there!
Is Delirium up your marble stair?"

"I know that both you and my sister have a burning desire."
The prince/ss said coolly. And it reached down and added a
small, scarlet heart to the chain Barnabas carried in his mouth.
"This will help you with our sister."

"What's *that* supposed to mean?" the puppy yapped.
"Is someone gonna tell me how to *use* these things?
Can *you* tell me where Delirium *is*?"

The sibling began, "I suggest you ask our...."

"I know! I know!...ask your other brother..." finished Barnabas grumpily.
"Lemme just rest for a minute...yawn...
and I'll be on my way...zzZZZ..."

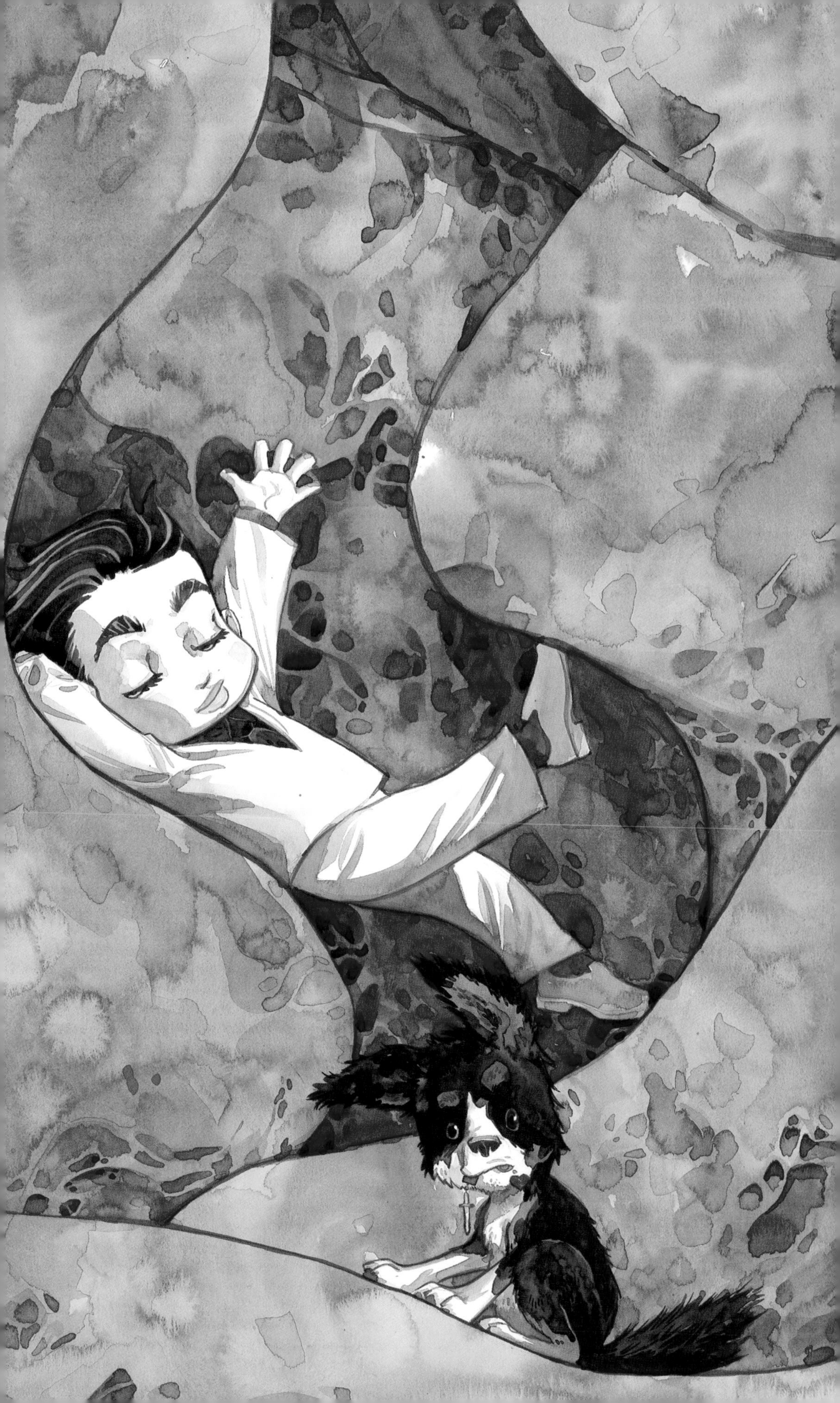

"...ZZzzZ!"

A moment later the frazzled pup found himself in The Dreaming,
where people go when they fall asleep.
Delirium's older brother Dream ruled the land here,
surrounded by the Almost Things.

Barnabas frisked through the fields of fresh dog biscuits.
Balls bounced past him as he sampled the succulent, bone-laden bushes.
He chased zippy cars along hydrant-laced streets and wagged his tail as
the Dream Things scratched and scratched behind his ears.

"Thanks, guys! I needed that! It feels wonderf...what the heck?
Did you guys see that? Something just zipped past me.
And now on the other side! Did you see it?"

The little black bird just fluttered above his head,
but the pumpkin boy took a deep breath and said,
"It's about time someone asked fer my opinion! There's too many
somethin's zipping around here, if ya ask me! They make a lotta mess
and scatter the whatsamajiggits all willy-nilly! And do they tear up the
Anythings! Yeesh! An' who has ta clean that mess up?
Yer lookin' at him, pally! An' another thing...."

Barnabas readied himself and tucked his tail in preparation to take off.
"O-kay! How about you guys stall it while I get a head start?"

And off he zoomed to Dream's castle.

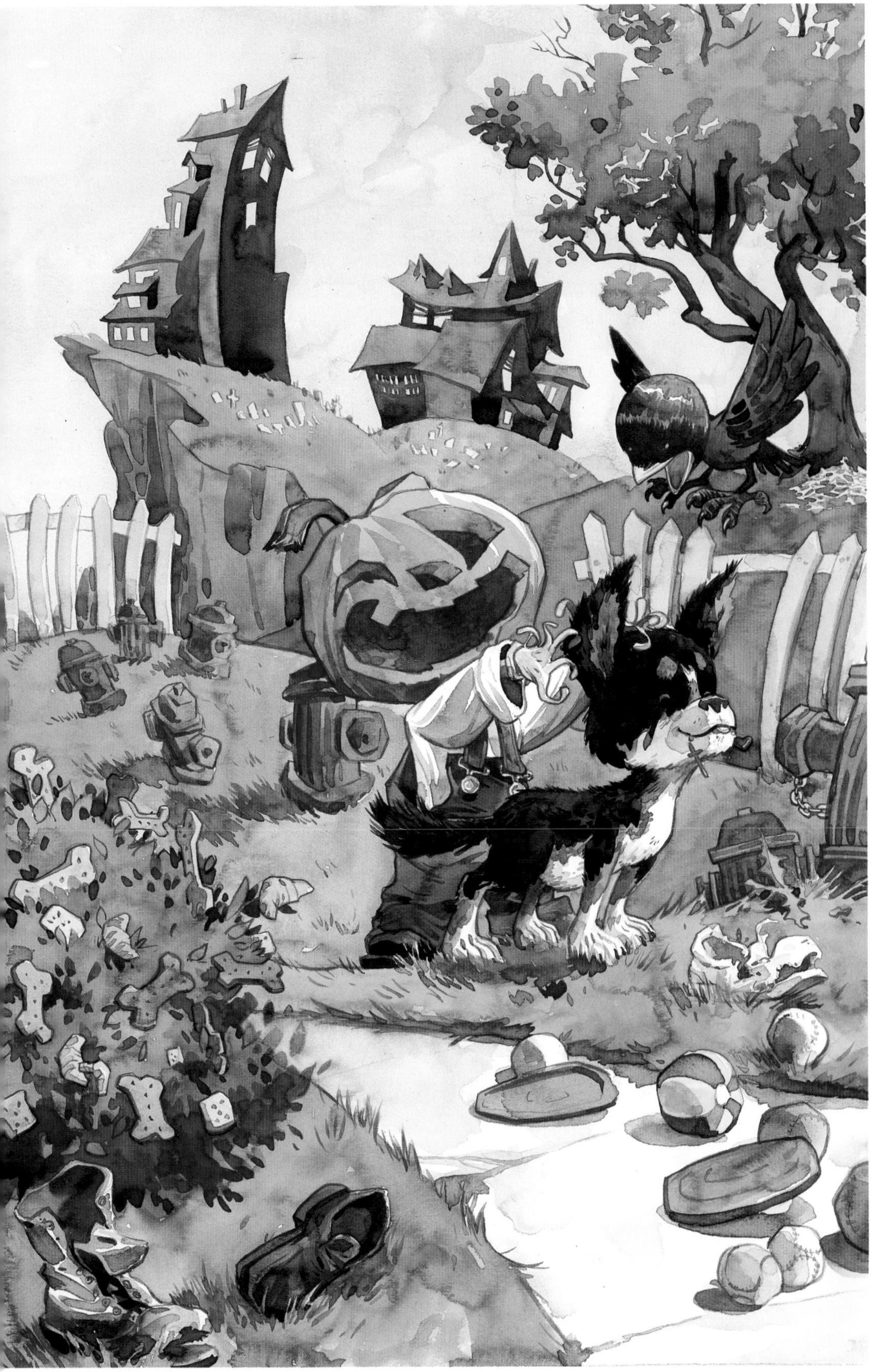

The Lord of Dreams was sitting upon his midnight throne
when the desperate dog approached him.

"My Lord, could you help me locate your youngest sister?
I've looked and looked but I haven't been able to find her!" barked Barnabas.

"She is not asleep, little dog, so she is not visiting my realm,"
replied the brother.

"*That* helps me..." muttered the pup.

Barnabas jangled when he spoke, and the charms glittered
in the moonlight as they hung from his mouth.

The little king took the chain of charms and placed a star upon the end.
"Here," he said. "Take this. It will help you with my sister."

"Great! Is anybody ever gonna tell me *how* this is gonna help me with her?
'Specially since she isn't *here*?" yapped the exasperated dog.

"I suggest you ask our oldest sister,"
stated the Prince of the Evening.

"Of course you do..." retorted Barnabas with vinegar.
Then, he journeyed on.

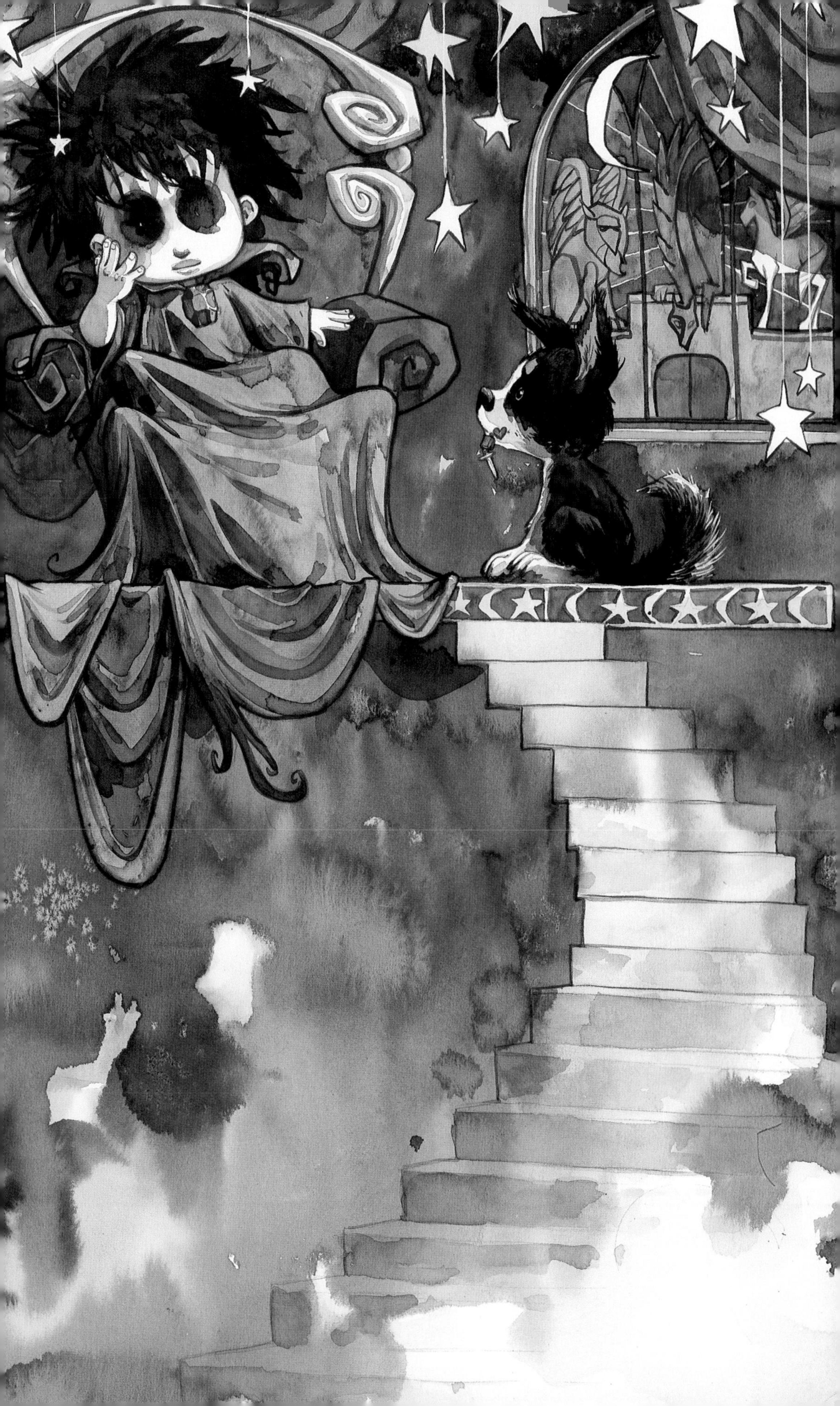

Barnabas crept through the nothingness.
He might have walked for an hour or he might have trekked for a day.
You never could tell in *this* realm.
But Barnabas was determined
to keep moving until he found Delirium.
It was then that he realized only one sibling remained:
The Oldest sister! Oh *no!* What if Delirium was there with *her!*
She'd be forever in the Nothing!

He shivered and tucked his tail between his legs and slowly carried on.

*F*inally, Barnabas emerged from the Empty
and stood before Delirium's oldest sister
who was sitting upon a divan in her apartment suite.

"My Lady," he whispered.
"I am looking for your youngest sister, the little Lady Delirium.
I fear I have lost her forever..."

The oldest of the Endless family smiled sweetly
at Delirium's frightened friend.

"Little Barnabas, my sister is not here with me,
so she is not lost to you," she informed him.

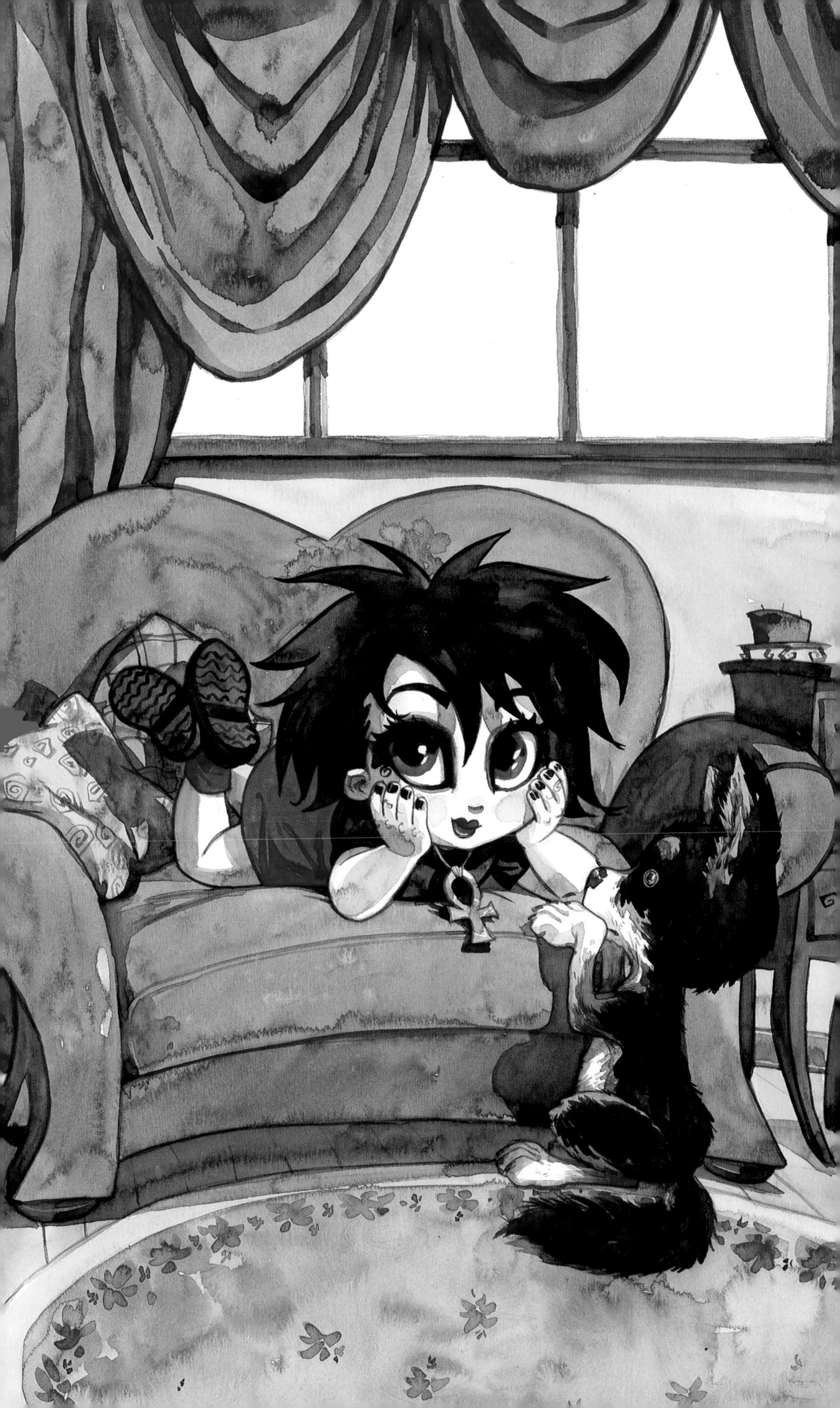

"*R*eally? *Oh, thank you!*" he barked as he skipped and twirled in happiness. "That's great news!"

As he swirled a second time, he could swear he saw that Thing that had been on his trail throughout the whole quest.

This was too much!

Finally, Barnabas felt brave enough to confront it once and for all!

"I've had enough of you!" he cried.

"I'm gonna catch you and see why you've been following me! So there!"

The oldest sister giggled as Barnabas chased the Thing, but it was always just out of his reach.

Round and round and round he went as the chain of charms flew out of his mouth. One by one, Delirium's oldest sister picked them up and added a tiny silver ankh to the other charms.

After fifty revolutions, Barnabas reached his breaking point and opened his jaws wide and—

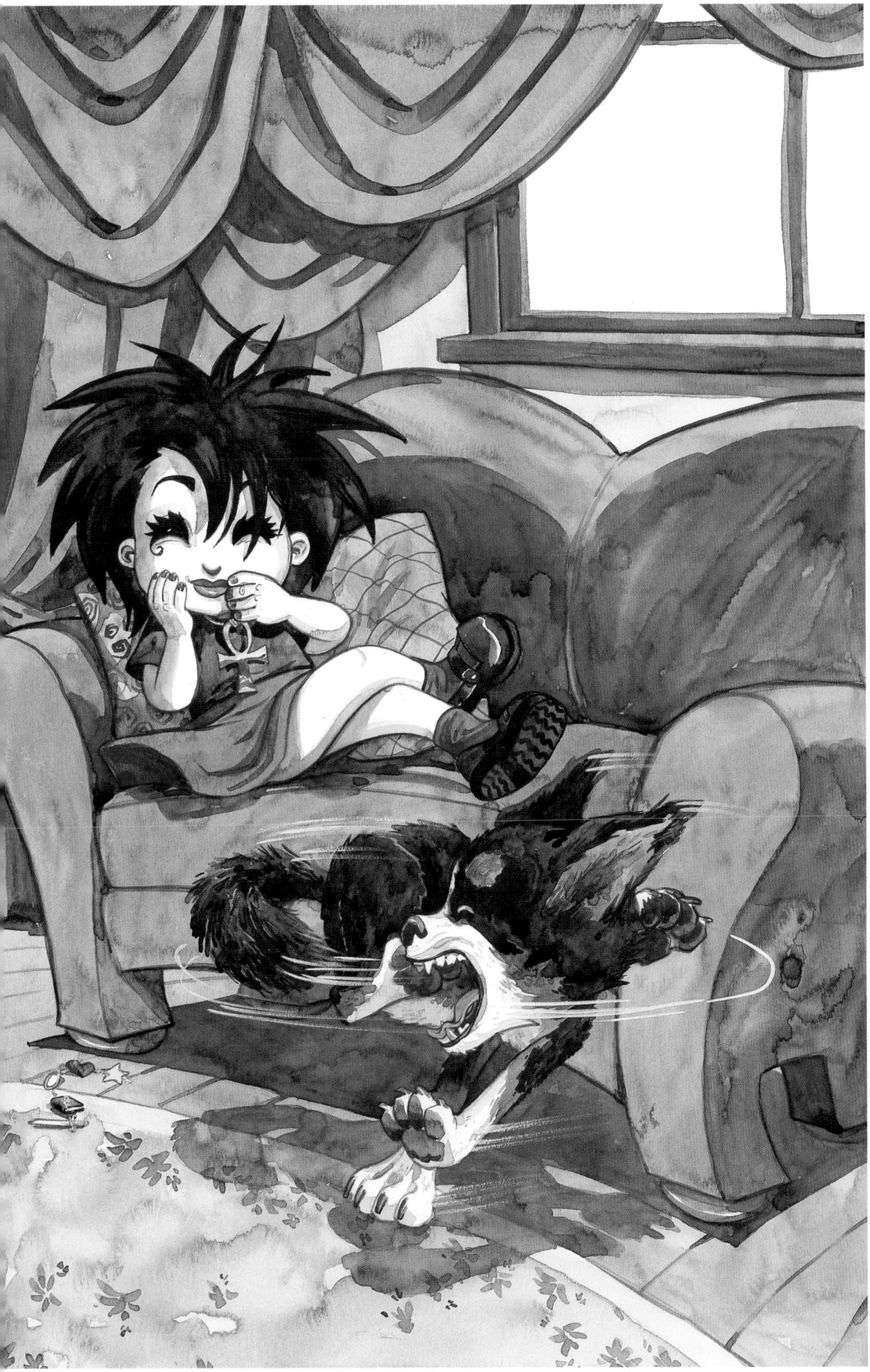

Snap! Success!

The oldest sister grinned as Barnabas came to a halt with his *tail* between his teeth. He was dizzy and the room was spinning. He had chased his tail until he was absolutely Delirious!

So Barnabas sang:

"All around the foozberry bush,
the fuzzy chased the twinkle ...
Round and round and up and down...
Where is my twinkle?"

"Right here next to you—you bad doggie!" said the princess Delirium.

And suddenly, she was!

"I'm so glad you're where I didn't remember I put you!
And I've been looking and looking.
Don't ever get losted from me again!"

Delirium hugged her puppy tightly.

"Easier said than done, kiddo!" he yipped.

"I'll say!" agreed Delirium's oldest sister as she handed Barnabas the circle of charms. "Here, this will help you with our sister," she whispered in his ear.

"Bye-Bye, big sister, it's time for us to go home!" Delirium said as she tugged at her puppy's tail. "Mr. Doggie, promise me you'll never go out walky walking without a leashie!"

"I promise," replied Barnabas with a wink.

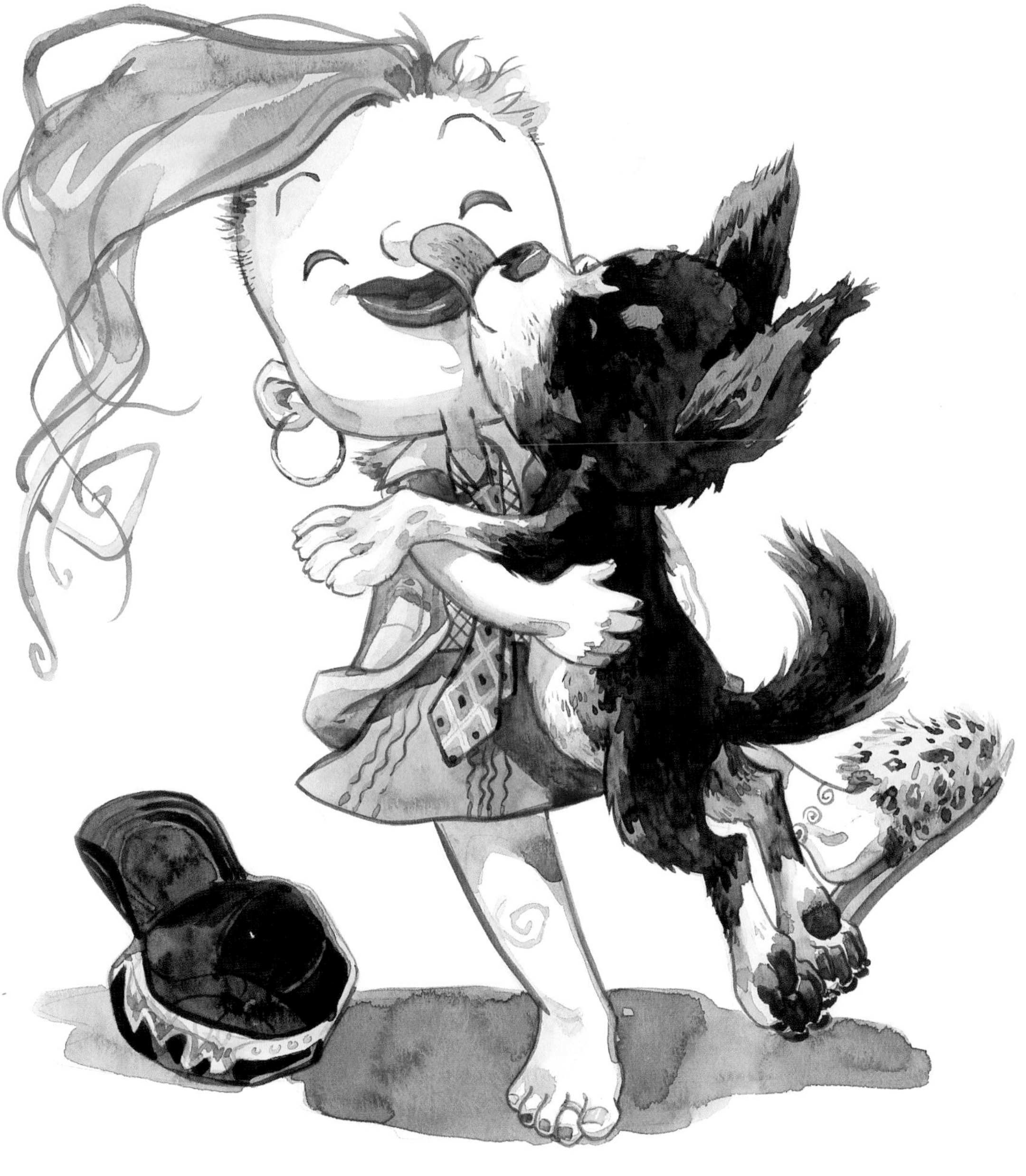

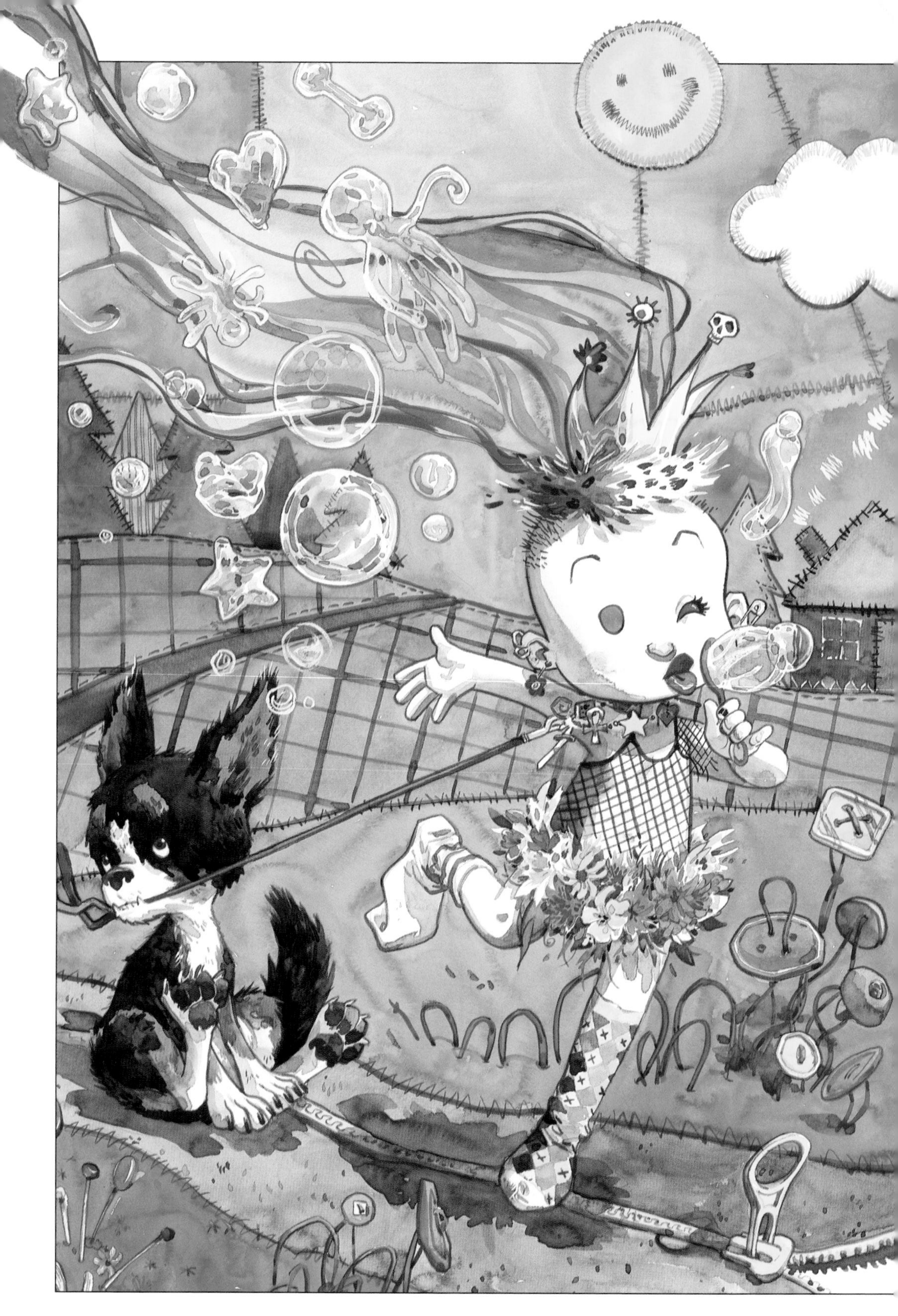

Once upon a time, in a champagne-bubbly realm, there lived a tiny princess named Delirium and her dog Barnabas. It was Barnabas' job to look after the fizzy princess because she was very easily distracted and often got lost if she went walking by herself.

The End

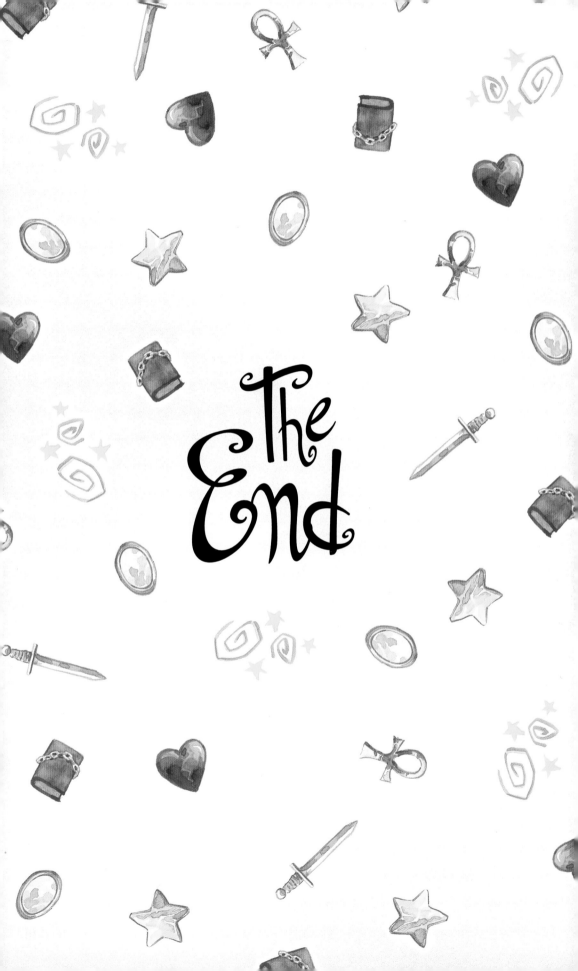

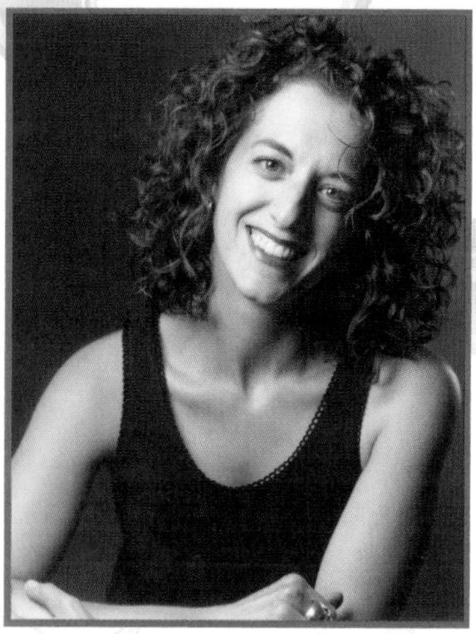

JILL THOMPSON

reveals the secret history of the Little Endless!

INSPIRATION

I was working on the SANDMAN series with N Gaiman, specifically on a story called "T Parliament of Rooks." Neil wrote a passage wh one character tells a story about when Death a

DREAM AND DEATH IN THE SANDMAN #40.

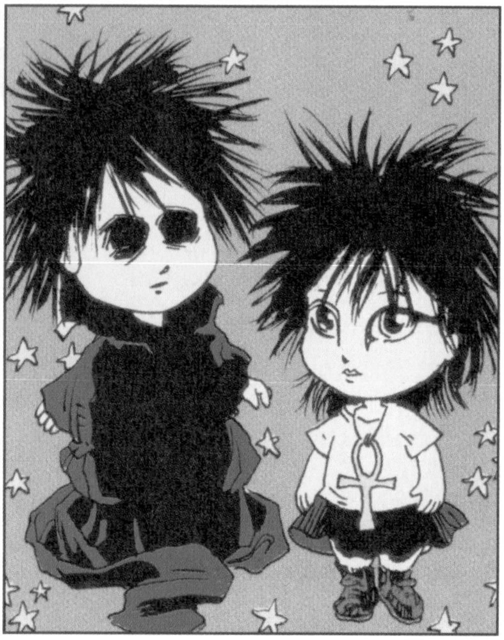

Dream of the Endless were children. Neil h wanted it to be an homage to the DC Com characters *Sugar and Spike*, but I decid to give them more of a Japanese cutene

WHO CAME FIRST

Once Death and Dream appeared in diminu tive form in issue #40 of THE SANDMAN they quickly became the most requeste sketches from fans. Then I decided t "shrink" the other Endless. I faxed a draw ing to Neil and proceeded to paint a Littl Endless family portrait. The fans wen crazy. They wanted to see postcards o posters and books that featured the "little" Endless family.

THE FIRST FAMILY PORTRAIT OF THE LITTLE ENDL

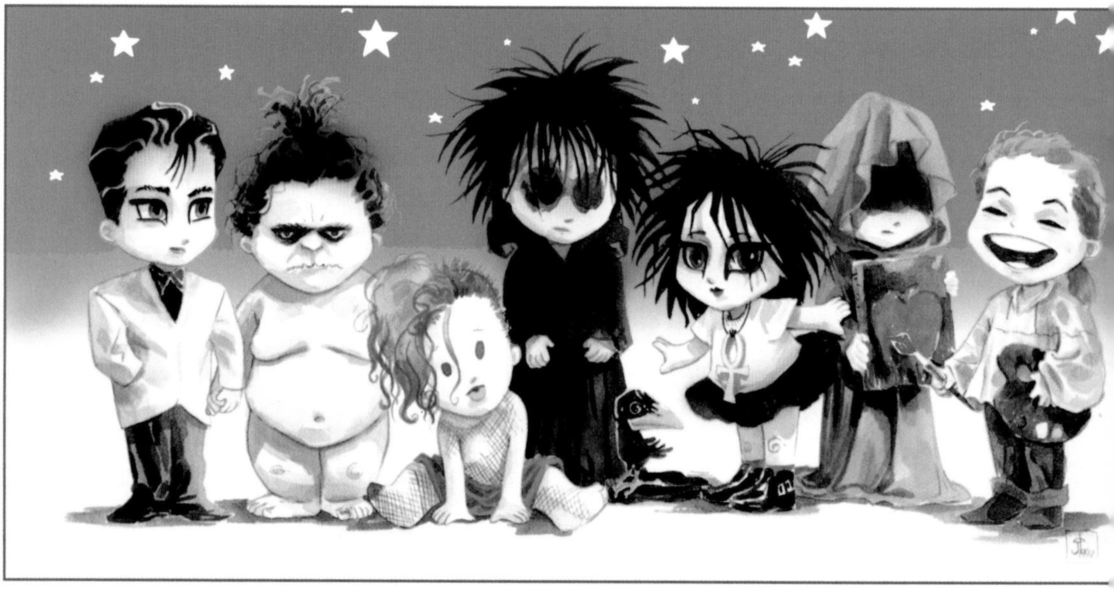

›LL CRAZY

·afted some little stuffed dolls Dream and Death in 1993. ewed a little black dress for ıth and a cloak for Dream. ;ed an ankh necklace I had for ıth's ankh so it looked really ·rsized, and I painted their es. It took me two days to · on their yarn hair. Fans wanted me to make dolls them, but it was too much work for one person. ›ld everyone interested to write to DC and ask for ne plush merchandise. DC Direct eventually produced eries of plush Little Endless many years after I made ›se first handmade dolls. Neil Gaiman has the original ls, and writer Paul Dini has the only other handmade r I sewed. I designed all the character turnarounds them.

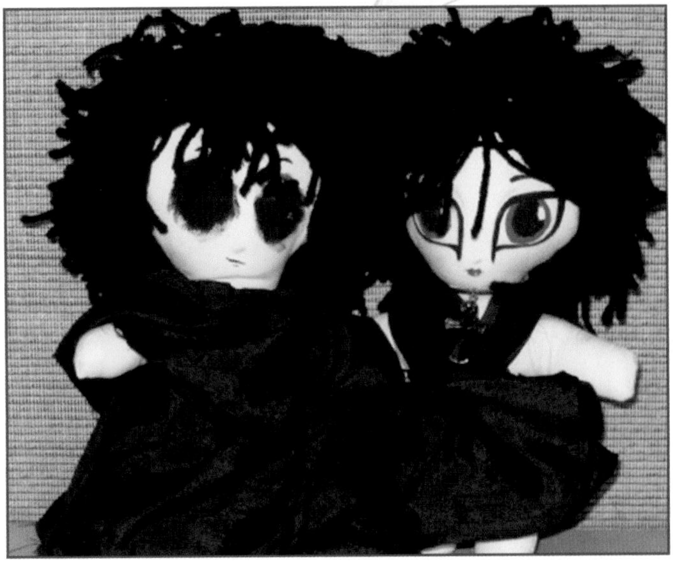

JILL'S ORIGINAL HANDMADE DOLLS.

TTLE DEATH ;. DEATH

·'s very giggly when she's le — kind of chubby and e like a gothic kewpie doll.

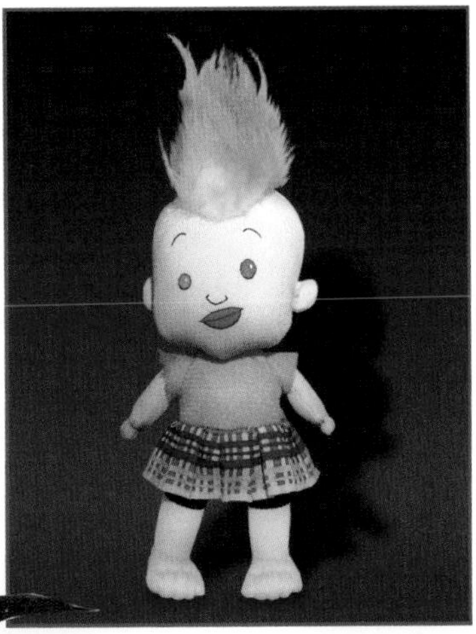

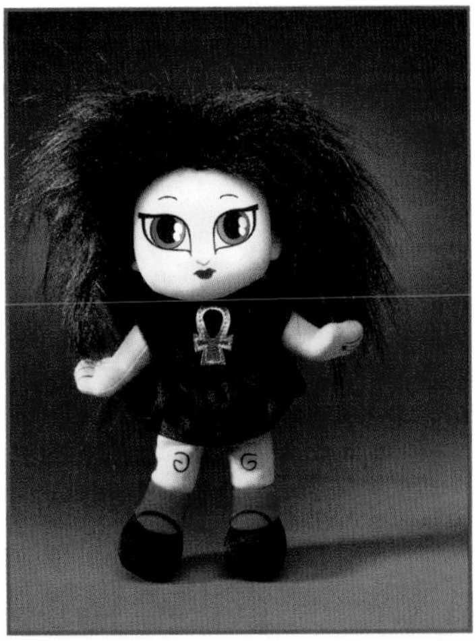

LITTLE DELIRIUM, LITTLE DEATH, LITTLE MORPHEUS & LITTLE DANIEL ARE ALL APPROXIMATELY 8" TALL.

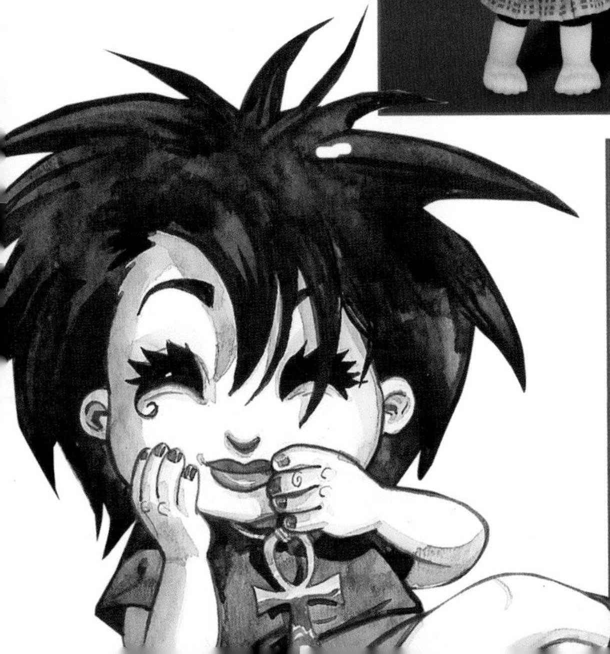

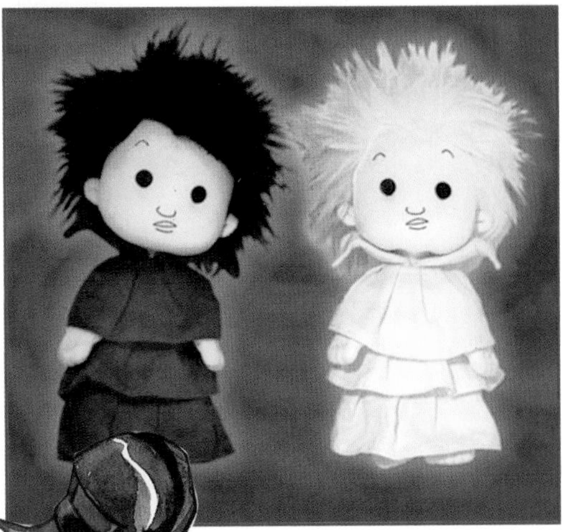

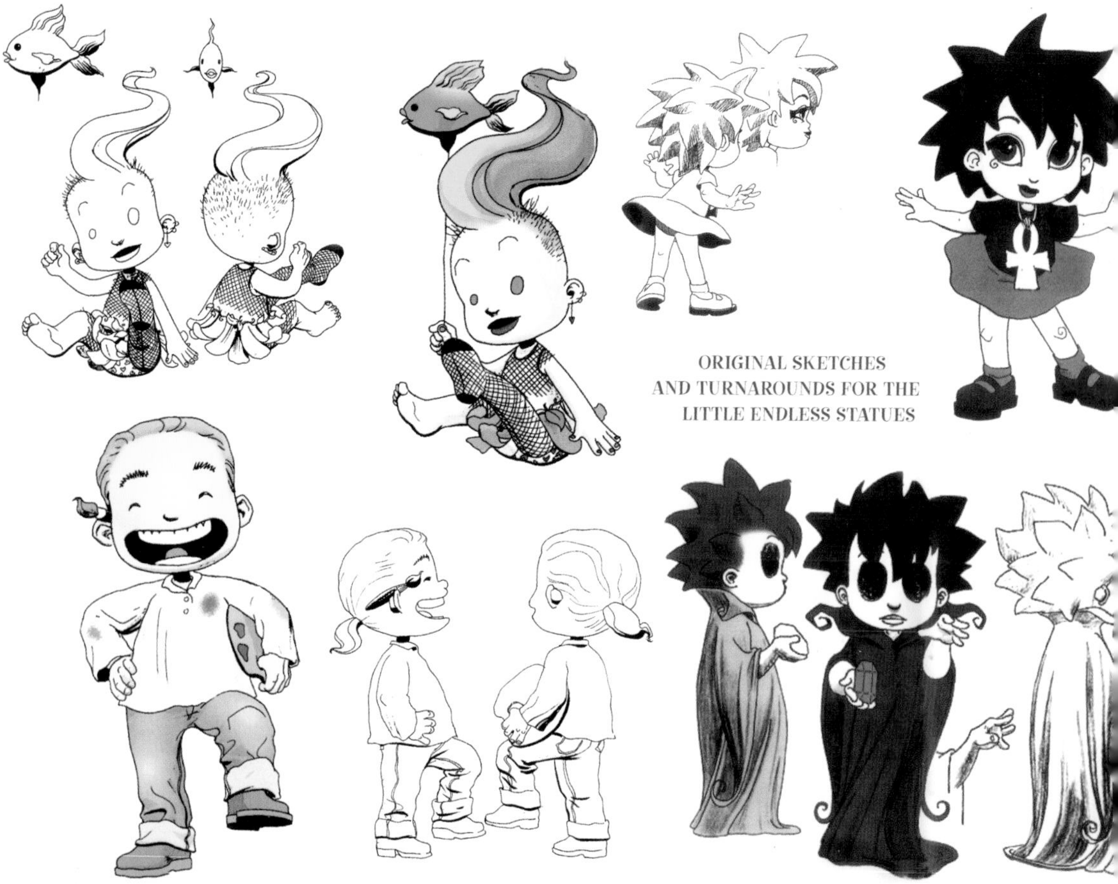

ORIGINAL SKETCHES
AND TURNAROUNDS FOR THE
LITTLE ENDLESS STATUES

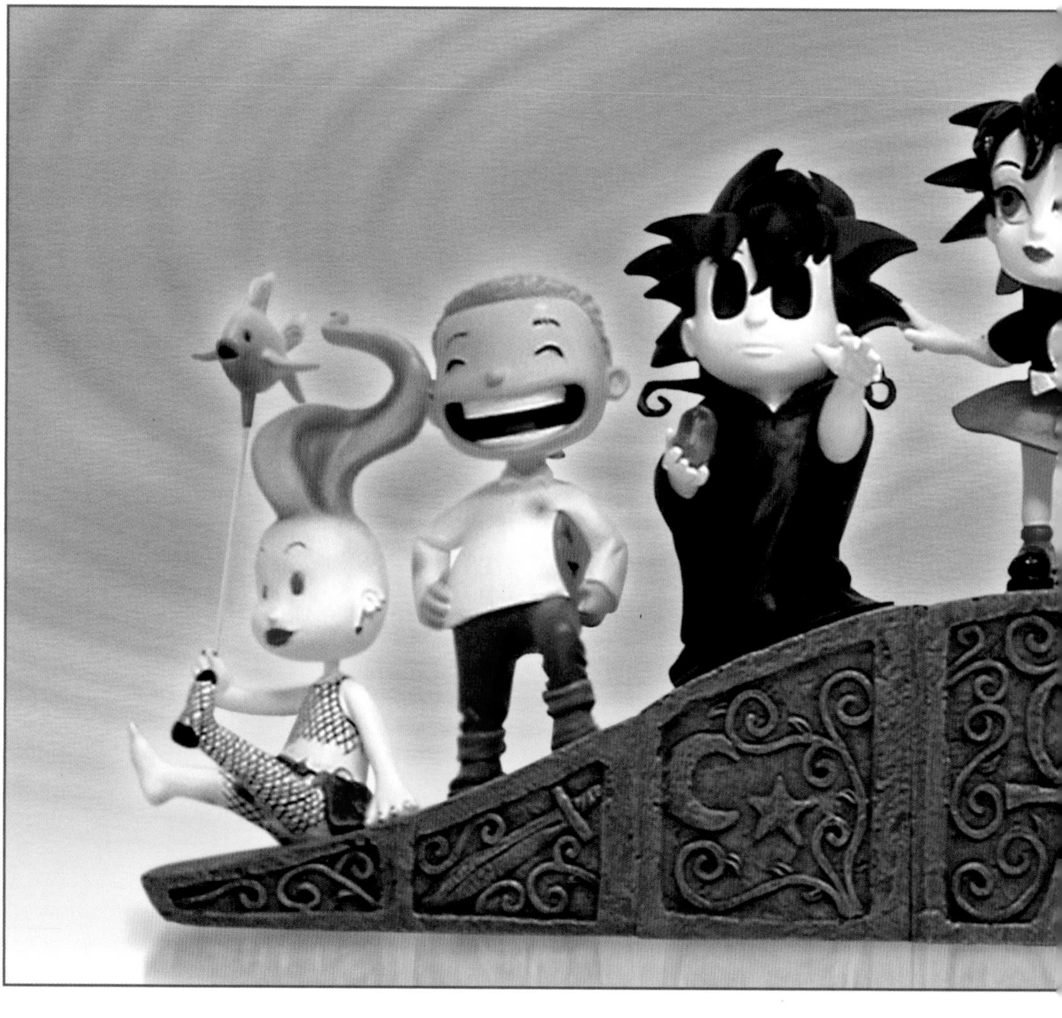

ATUES

:signed all the racter turnarounds for Little Endless statues. statues were amazingly lpted by Barsom and duced in 2003.

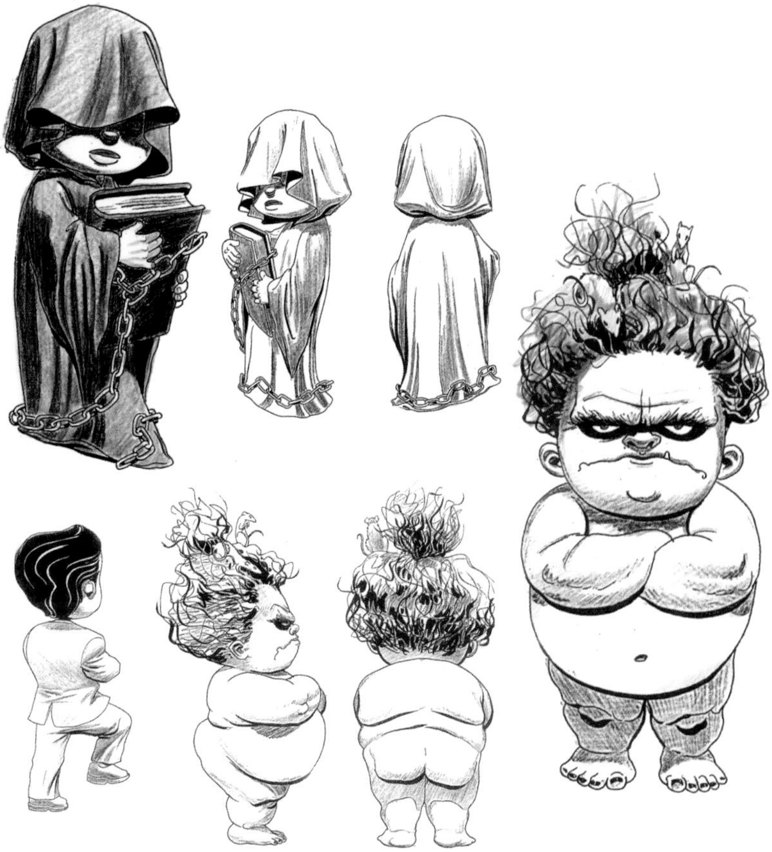

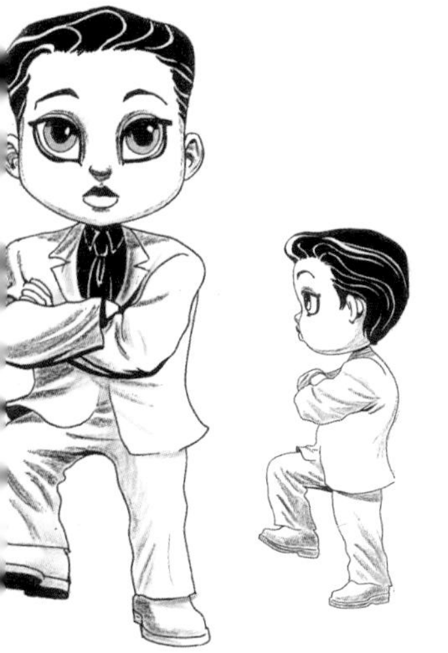

THE LITTLE ENDLESS STATUES CAN BE DISPLAYED AS SHOWN OR SEPARATELY.

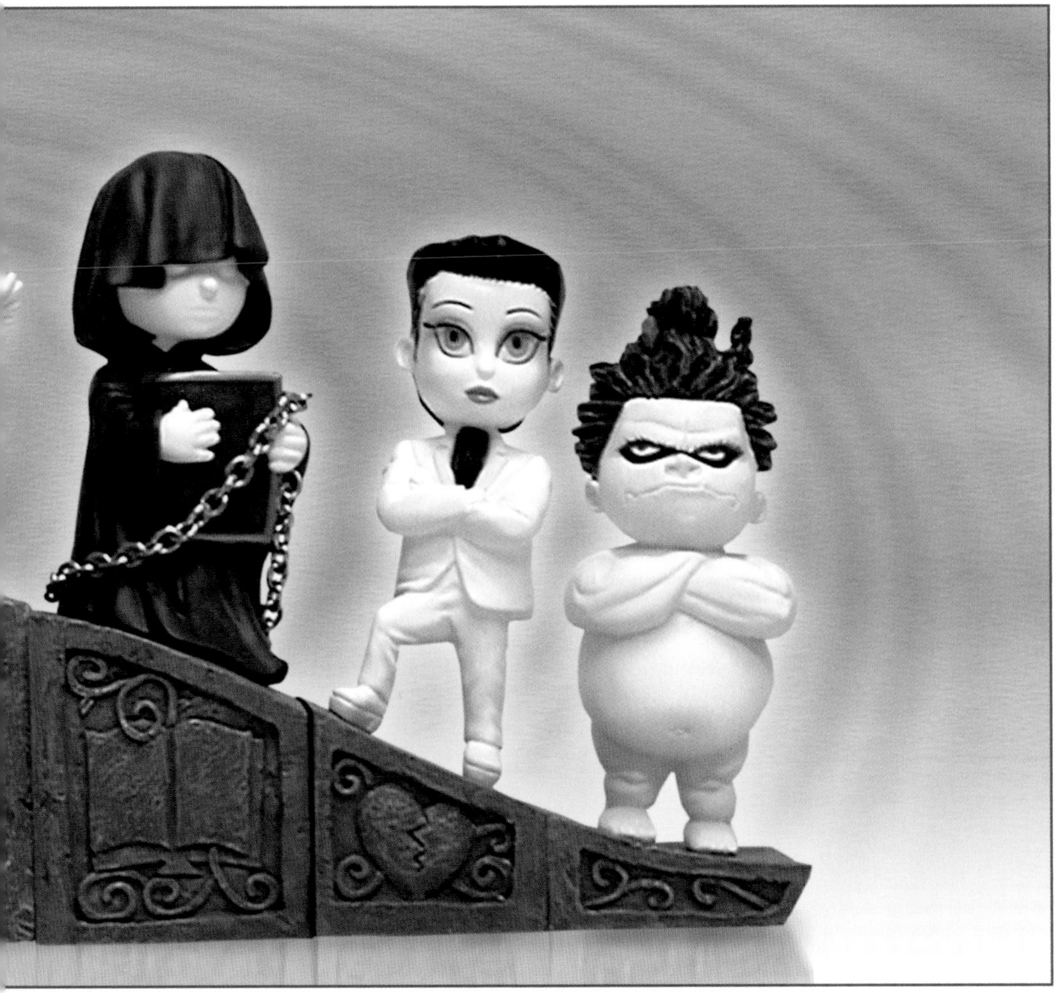

FAVORITES

Hmm. I like them all, but I really like drawing Despair in the super-deformed manner. She looks so funny, it cracks me up. I also love Delirium.

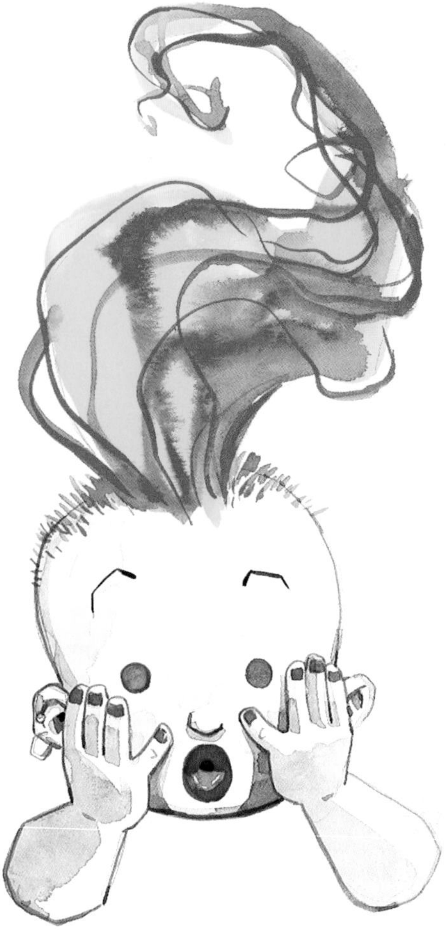

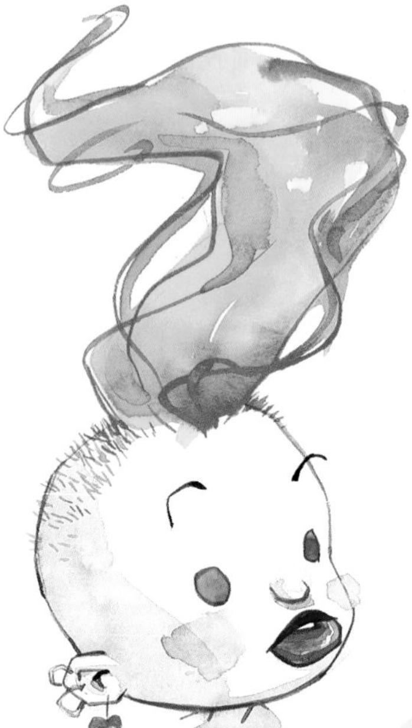

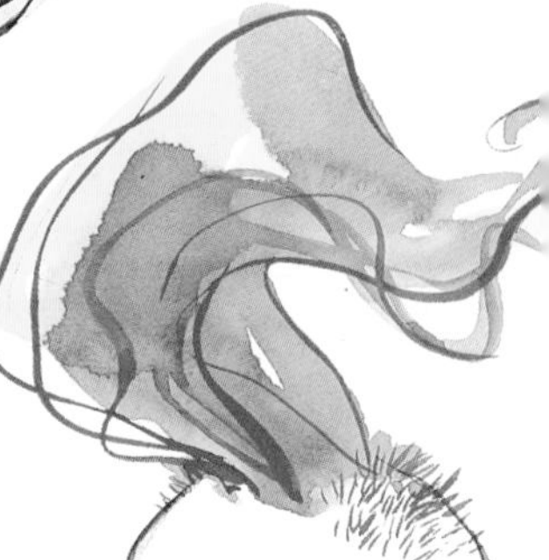

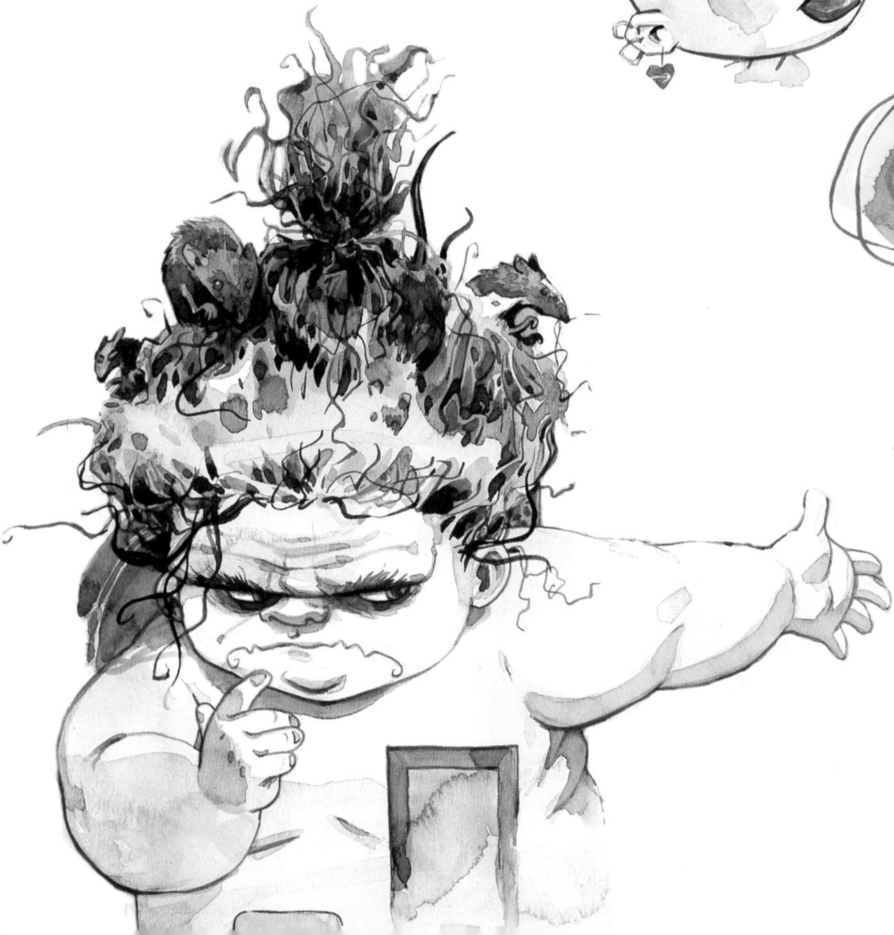

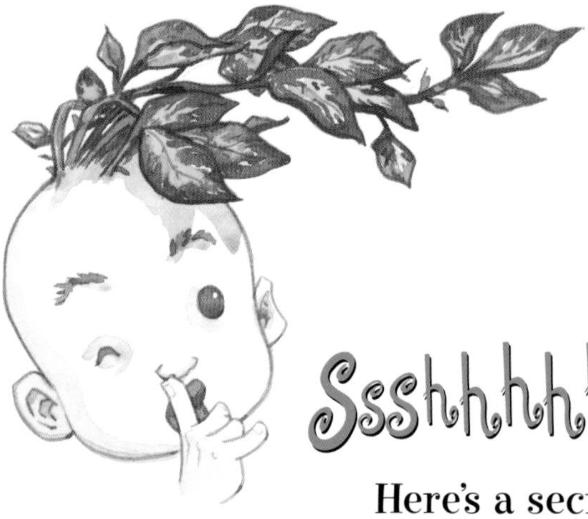

Ssshhhhh! Ssshhhhh!

Here's a secret preview of
DELIRIUM'S PARTY:
A LITTLE ENDLESS STORYBOOK!

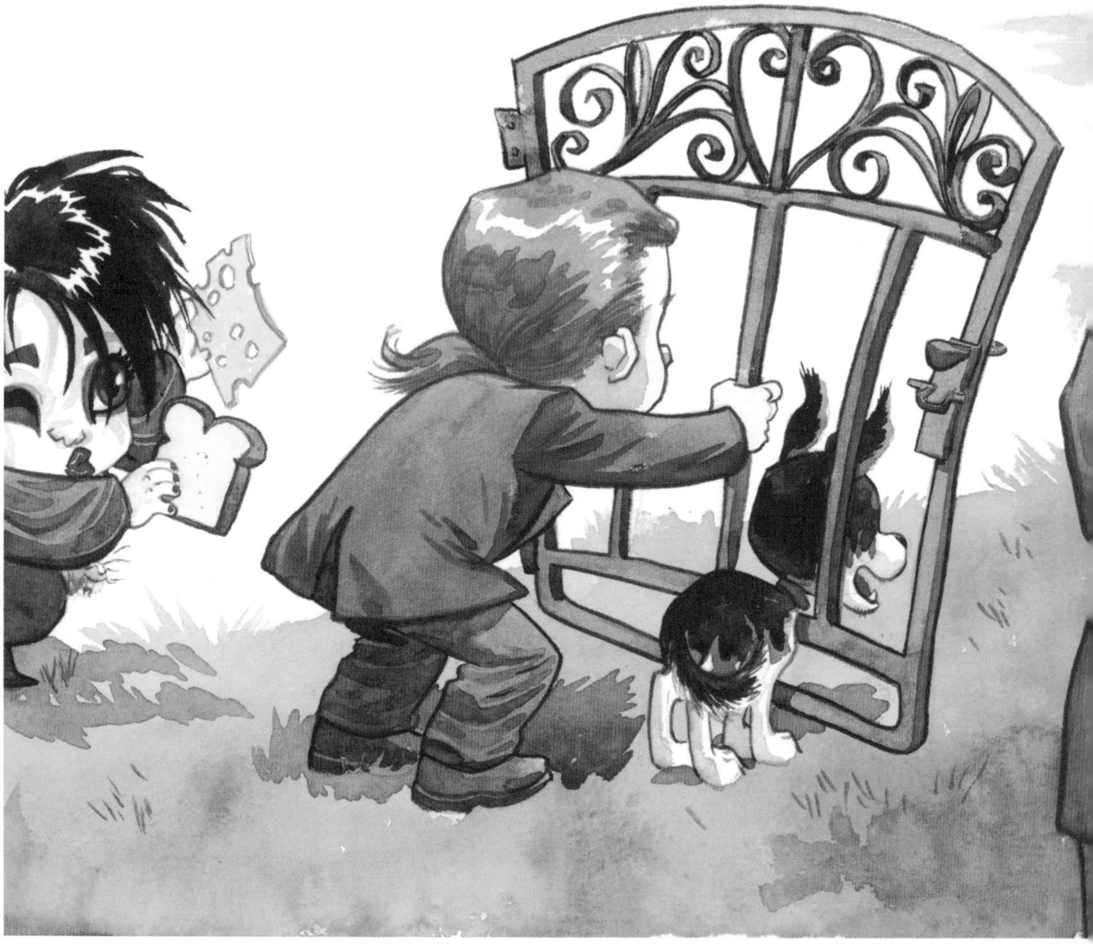

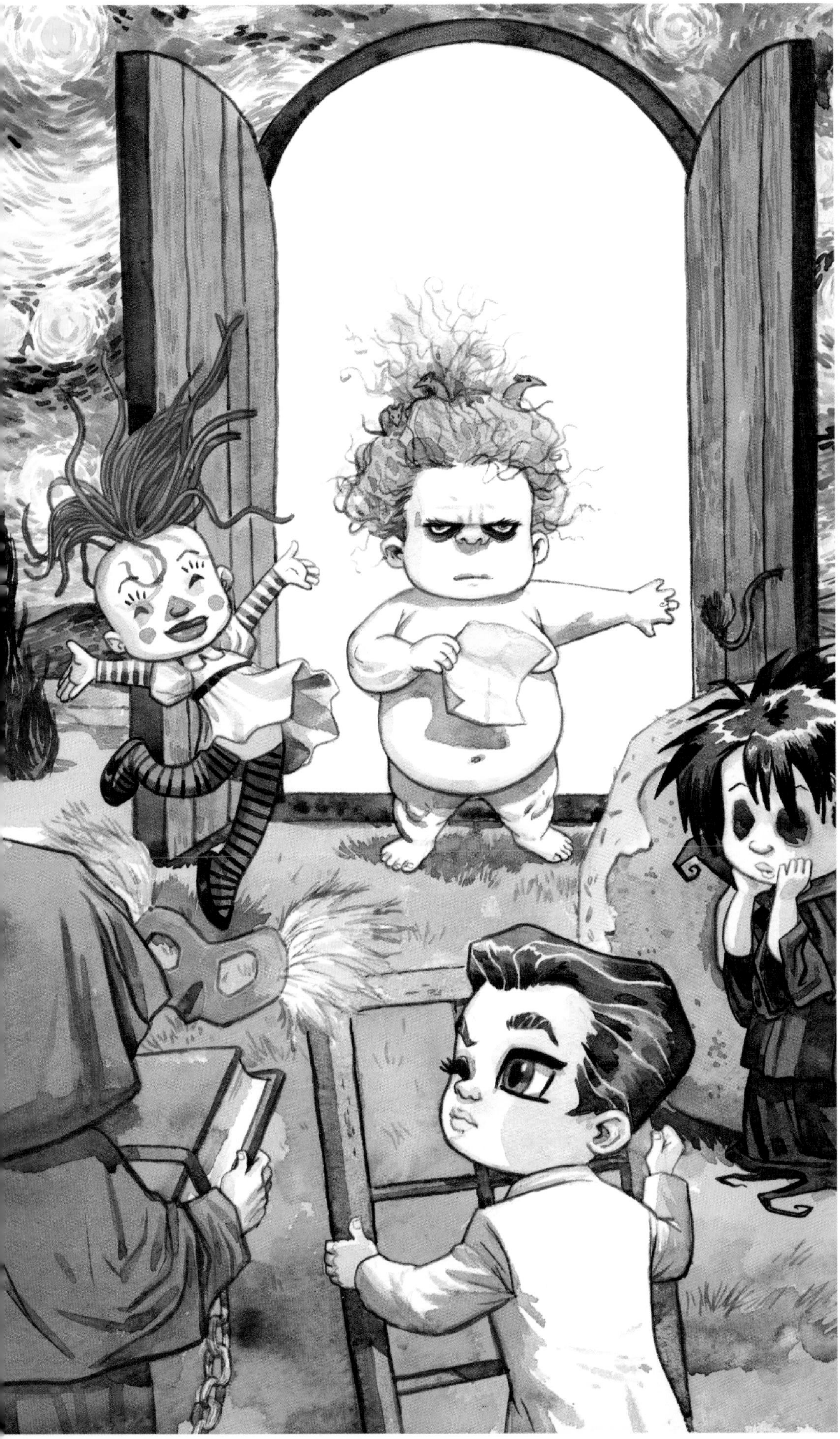

JILL THOMPSON is a comic book illustrator and the creator of *Scary Godmother* and *Magic Trixie*. She's been working in the comic book industry for quite a long time and really, really likes it there. She is a graduate of the American Academy of Art in Chicago. She has been fortunate to win multiple Eisner Awards for her comics work.

Jill has collaborated with various amazing authors over the years such as Neil Gaiman, Grant Morrison, Will Pfeifer, Evan Dorkin and Mick Foley. If you'd like to check out works other than this fine book by Jill, try these collaborative efforts — *The Sandman: Brief Lives*, *The Invisibles*, *Wonder Woman*, *Finals*, *Beasts of Burden*, Mick Foley's *Halloween Hijinx* and *Tales from Wrescal Lane*.

For work written and illustrated by Jill and Jill alone, sample Vertigo's *At Death's Door*, *The Dead Boy Detectives*, *Delirium's Party: A Little Endless Storybook* and, of course, the *Scary Godmother* series and *Magic Trixie* series.

When not creating stories, Jill enjoys making things, cooking stuff, traveling around the US and beyond meeting her fans and speaking about literacy, comics and art. Oh yeah — and having a good time. And smiling. Lots of smiling.

Follow her on Twitter @thejillthompson

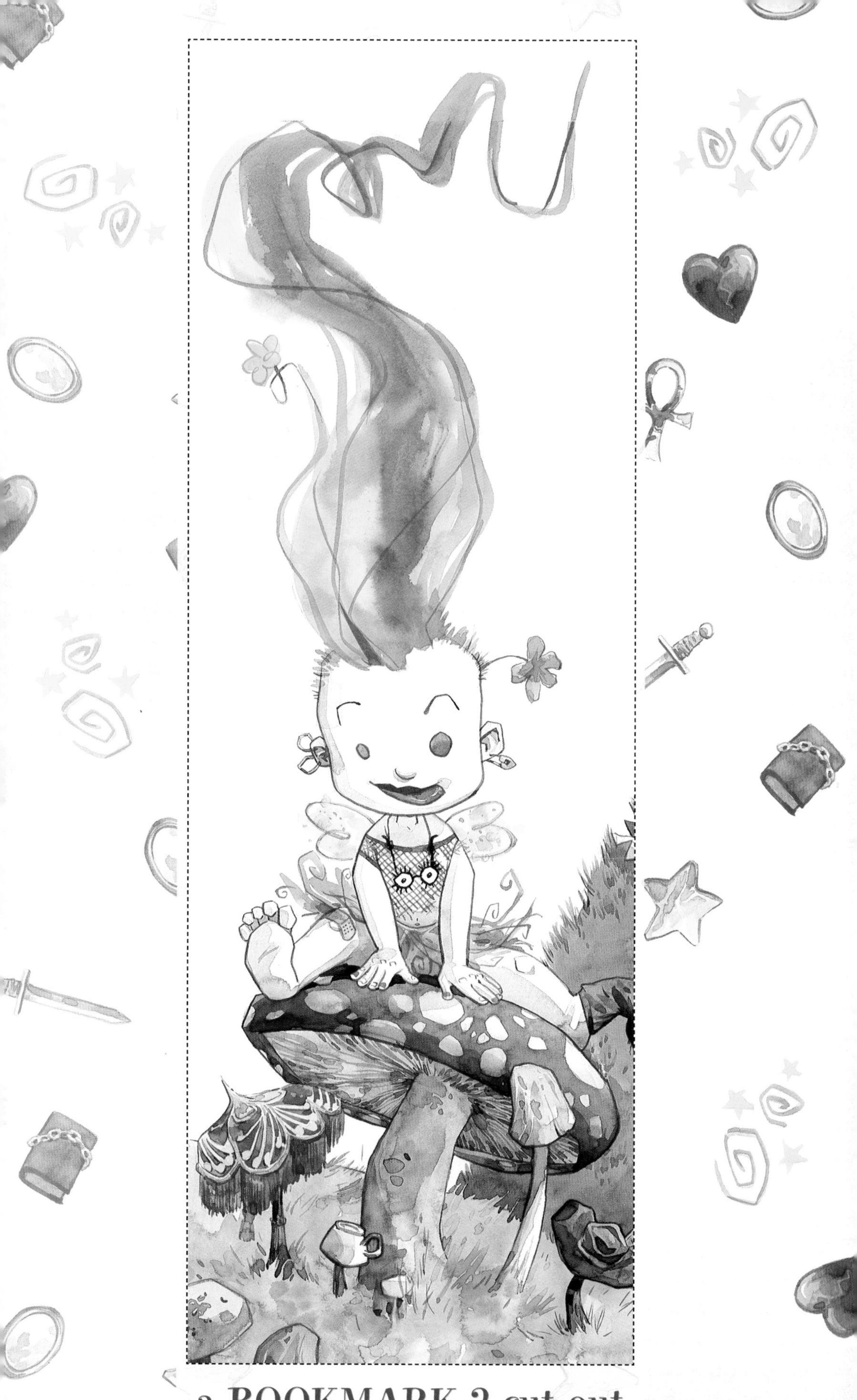

a BOOKMARK 2 cut out